Christmas 2009

Betty Ruth's
home in Greenville.
Her father was
a medical doctor

Papa

Come Cook With Me

Come Cook With Me

Betty Ruth

TWO HARBORS PRESS

MINNEAPOLIS

Two Harbors Press
212 3rd Avenue North, Suite 290
Minneapolis, MN 55401
612.455.2293
www.TwoHarborsPress.com

First Edition

ISBN - 978-1-935097-74-7
ISBN - 1-935097-74-1
LCCN - 2009936878

Book sales for North America and international:
Itasca Books, 5120 Cedar Lake Road, Minneapolis, MN 55416
Phone: 952.345.4488 (toll free 1.800.901.3480)
Fax: 952.920.0541; email to orders@itascabooks.com

Cover Design and Typeset by Kristeen Wegner

Printed in the United States of America

Table of Contents

Acknowledgements

Cover: My good friend and colleague (physician turned artist) Don Stewart very kindly gave me permission to use one of his incredible ballpoint composites that I found on his website www.dsart.com. His caduceus filled with fruits and vegetables symbolizes the two loves of my life, cooking and medicine. He, also, allowed me to have color added. Julia Greer, a talented young artist added the color and Jim at Grapevine Graphics, Inc. printed my cover. Caroline Azzi of Marbella, Spain (www.carolineazzi.com), while studying with the artist NALL (www.nallart.com), did my most flattering portrait on the back cover and presented it to me as a gift. I especially want to thank Kristeen Wegner, Michelle Brown, Jenni Wheeler, Danielle Adelman and Anna Schmeling of Mill City Press. They have been so very patient and helpful in guiding this neophyte through her publication.

Without the advice , encouragement, and support of my friends Bettie McGowin Miller, Ann-Clinton Groom, Judy Barnes, Sue Brannon Walker and Beppie Boykin, my dream of a cookbook would never have come to fruition.

Dedication

To Elmira Sanders, who patiently taught me to cook when I was a child. I spent many happy hours standing beside her in our kitchen. She fed a country doctor's family well for many, many years. Her recipes remain the best!

And, to all of those who have so kindly endured my culinary efforts over the years. A special thank you to Patrick, who eats every meal away from home. If he calls and I say "I'm cooking!" and he accepts an impromptu invitation, I know that he will critically judge my meal "a keeper" or "one of your worst."

Cooking and giving repast to friends is one of the greatest pleasures of my life. Perhaps it is a selfish gift; because, planning and executing a party is one of the most therapeutic and satisfying activities with which I indulge myself.

Dear friends, who have eaten, not only at table, but on the floor, in the kitchen, the bed, emergency rooms, surgical suites, morgues, etc., etc. I thank you.

Introduction

At long last this "gyne-gourmand" has time to play in her kitchen, entertain, and write her cookbook. Finding myself alone many years ago, after a busy day in surgery or the office, I would not allow myself to pick up supper, buy packaged or prepared meals at the market, nor live on sandwiches and peanut butter. I soon found that preparing a three or four-course dinner each evening was most entertaining and a better tranquilizer than any available pharmaceutical product. I have always been a scratch cook and known that no dish is better than when prepared with fresh produce and meats.

Being a munchkin, having long passed the age at which an extra calorie added inches overnight and having been born with a voracious appetite, I have had to learn to alter many of these recipes for my own consumption. For instance, I have come up with substitutions such as a package of Goya ham seasoning for ham hocks or bacon, low-fat milk for ½ and ½ , low-fat yogurt for sour cream, or simply a reduction of the amount of butter. Realizing that I could not just give you ingredients and directions without adding anecdotes, suggested accoutrements , sources, tips and suggestions, I offer you a cooktrek rather than a traditional cookbook. I love cookbooks and think of them as I do a roll of film - if I find one good picture out of an entire roll that I have snapped, I never cry over the many that are dreadful. Therefore, I hope that you find at least one recipe that you like in my little book. It will make me happy to know that I have shared one of my greatest pleasures.

If you are looking for "quickie recipes," this book is not for you! However, you will find some "quickie meals," because I gallop and frequently invite friends on the spur of the moment. I keep my freezer and pantry filled with "a kitchen supper" that can be served two hours after I extend the invitation. Please join me on this journey.

A meal or a party is so much more than carefully following precise recipe instructions. Food must satisfy all the senses: taste, sight, smell, and even auditory.

Many of these recipes are treasures that I have prepared - some for over six decades. Many were first prepared under the direction of my beloved Elmira, who would elevate me on a stool in her kitchen as a child, teach me, encourage me, and bless me as I struggled to learn.

Nothing delights me more than when a departing guest requests a recipe for a dish I have served. I have almost 3,000 recipes in my computer (some original and the others that I have prepared and added to my "keepers"). I frequently alter recipes when I find improvements during repeated preparations. I have tried many different recipe programs and have been most pleased with Now You're Cooking! You can purchase and download this great software at http://www.ffts.com .

I welcome guests in my kitchen while I am preparing and serving a meal or party, but never after dinner. After my guests depart, I carefully note "what is left" on plates or in serving dishes. Empty plates are a grand indicator of guest satisfaction. I much prefer to serve buffet style so no one is forced to twiddle, diddle, and attempt to hide a distasteful dollop that I have delivered on their plate.

Among my favorite cookbooks are Cooking for Mr. Latte, Christopher Blake's Easy Elegance Cookbook (old New Orleans recipes), San Francisco À La Carte, The Phantom Cookbook, Jubilee (the original one), Seconds Please, Cooking in the Nude and my Gourmet compendiums.

If you have questions or find the directions for a recipe unclear, please contact me amsac@gyne.com !

Peeps

A Peep in my Pantry

Olives - Kalamata and basic pitted stuffed with pimientos

BRS Lemon Vinaigrette

Flour - plain and bread machine (prefer King Arthur flours)

Homemade bread mix

Pastas-angel hair, linguine, spinach

Canned diced tomatoes, tomato sauce, tomato paste and Rotel (original)

Canned chicken broth

Jello and plain gelatin

Yeast

Chocolate-squares and cocoa (prefer Droste)

Bouillon cubes - chicken, beef, ham, chicken and fish

Spices - cloves, cinnamon, allspice (whole and powdered), basil, sage, oregano, cumin, paprika, whole peppercorns, poultry seasoning, and saffron

Seasoning bases- ham, beef, veal and chicken

Yeast

Anchovies - canned and paste

Artichoke hearts and hearts of palm

Olive oil

Vinegar - plain and balsamic

Marmite

Evaporated milk - small cans for emergencies!

A Peep in My Refrigerator

Eggs

Milk

Pesto (homemade or Four Winds Deli)

Sun dried tomatoes in olive oil

Cheese (Edam, feta, cheddar, goat cheese, bleu cheese, fresh mozzarella,
and Parmesan)

Capers

Green peppercorns in brine

A Peep in My Freezer

Croustades

Spaghetti sauce

Lemon Curd

Gumbo

Turkey bone gumbo

Spicy pecans

Cheese straws

Oyster Rockefeller Sauce
- frozen in ice cube trays for instant Oysters Rockefeller

Fresh shrimp - frozen in water with heads on

Jezebel Sauce

Mushroom Turnovers (unbaked)

Individual Pesto Tortes

Favorite Kitchen Pots, Pans, and Gadgets

Tomato corer

Food loops (http://www.thefoodloop.com)

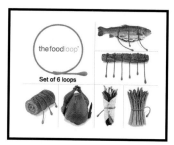 

Cherry pitter (great for olives!)

Bread machine (used only for mixing, kneading, and rising)

Asparagus peeler (Wms Sonoma)

Old iron skillets-well seasoned (never washed with soap!)

Le Creuset Dutch oven

Pop-up sponges

Olive oil jar with brush insert

Vol-au-vent cutters

Tagine

The History of Aprons

The principal use of Grandma's apron was to protect the dress underneath, because she only had a few; it was easier to wash aprons than dresses and they used less material., Along with that, it served as a potholder for removing hot pans from the oven.

It was wonderful for drying children's tears, and on occasion was even used for cleaning out dirty ears.

From the chicken coop, the apron was used for carrying eggs, fussy chicks, and sometimes half-hatched eggs to be finished in the warming oven.

When company came, those aprons were ideal hiding places for shy kids.

And when the weather was cold, grandma wrapped it around her arms.

Those big old aprons wiped many a perspiring brow, bent over the hot wood stove.

Chips and kindling wood were brought into the kitchen in that apron.

From the garden, it carried all sorts of vegetables. After peas had been shelled, it carried out the hulls.

In the fall, the apron was used to bring in apples that had fallen from the trees.

When unexpected company drove up the road, it was surprising how much furniture that old apron could dust in a matter of seconds.

When dinner was ready, Grandma walked out onto the porch, waved her apron, and the men knew it was time to come in from the fields to dinner.

Grandma used to set her hot baked apple pies on the window sill to cool.
Her granddaughters set theirs on the window sill to thaw.
They would go crazy now trying to figure out how many germs were on that apron.

I don't think I ever caught anything from an apron!
----Author Unknown

Appetizers

Spicy Pecans

1 pound pecans
¼ pound butter, melted
minced garlic
garlic salt
celery salt
red pepper
white pepper

Toast the pecans in a jelly roll pan in an oven preheated to 250° for 30 minutes. Continue toasting, stirring every 10 minutes just until pecans begin to brown. Pour the melted butter over the pecans and stir thoroughly. Sprinkle on celery salt, garlic salt, minced garlic and red pepper to taste. Toast 20 minutes longer, stirring occasionally. Sample a nut and if not toasted, continue cooking until lightly browned. Drain on brown paper (grocery bag) and season with white pepper and salt to taste. Freezes well.

Note: Toasting nuts should be a slow, drying process. If frozen, defrost briefly in microwave for emergency snacks!

Fromage

old cheeses, cubed
½ cup parsley, minced
1/4 cup white wine
2 tablespoons butter

Process all ingredients for 2 minutes and serve as a cheese spread.
Note: Save old ends and pieces of all cheeses in airtight bags. Should they
mold, trim off the mold. In just minutes you can make this tasty spread for
cocktail wafers or cucumber slices.

Braunsweiger Peppercorn Pâté

1 pound braunschweiger (liverwurst)
½ cup sour cream
½ pound mushrooms-minced
1 ¾ cups water
3 tablespoons clarified butter
¼ cup cognac
2 tablespoons minced parsley
1 package aspic mix (available at specialty stores or you can substitute
          Knox gelatin)
¾ teaspoon thyme
1 tablespoon peppercorns, packed in brine
¼ cup cognac
freshly ground black pepper to taste

Let Braunsweiger and sour cream come to room temperature and combine. Sauté the mushrooms in 3 tablespoons clarified butter until browned. Add parsley and thyme to mushrooms and sauté 1 minute. Place mushroom mixture in a bowl. Add cognac and freshly ground black pepper to taste. Combine mushroom and Braunsweiger mixtures. Pack in small crocks and pour a layer of cooled clarified butter over the pâté. Dissolve aspic in warmed brandy and water. Drain, saving peppered wine, and dot pâtés with peppercorns, then top with aspic and refrigerate.

To prepare peppercorns: Soak 1 tablespoon peppercorns (preferably mixed types) in ¾ jigger white wine overnight.

Note: Each holiday season I make these pâtés, place them in small levered Wick jars, and share them with friends.

Ceviche (or Seviche)

1 cup lime juice
1 ½ teaspoon salt
½ teaspoon Tabasco
2 lbs raw seafood (shrimp, conch or scallops)
2 tablespoons wine vinegar
⅓ cup olive oil
2 tomatoes, chopped
salt to taste
freshly ground black pepper
1 onion, chopped
1 clove garlic, minced
4 small chili peppers
1 bell pepper, chopped
1 rib celery, chopped
1 teaspoon cumin
1 teaspoon cilantro, chopped

In a large bowl, mix the lime juice, salt and tabasco. Add the small shrimp or diced seafood, stir gently, cover and marinate in refrigerator for at least 5 hours (preferably 24 hours). Toss the marinated seafood with a sauce made of tomatoes, onion, chilies, cilantro, oil, water and vinegar. Chill thoroughly before serving. Garnish with sliced avocado, if desired.

Note: I usually cook my seafood slightly (simmer for about 2 minutes in water or equal mixture of water and bottled clam juice) before placing it in the marinade.

Goat Cheese in Grape Leaves with Tomato and Olive Salad

½ cup olive oil
4 teaspoons chopped fresh thyme
¾ teaspoon freshly ground black pepper
12 large grape leaves from jar, rinsed, patted dry, stemmed
3 (4 oz) logs soft fresh goat cheese, each cut crosswise into 4 pieces
¼ cup extra-virgin olive oil
2 tablespoons balsamic vinegar
2 teaspoons Dijon mustard
⅓ cup coarsely chopped pitted oil-cured olives
6 ½ inch slices white bread; crusty style

Whisk ½ cup oil, thyme, and freshly ground black pepper in small bowl to blend. Arrange grape leaves, vein side up, on work surface. Dip each cheese round into thyme oil and place in center of 1 grape leaf. Fold sides of leaves over cheese; fold up bottom and continue to roll up, enclosing cheese completely. Arrange wrapped cheeses, seam side down, on platter. Brush lightly with some thyme oil. Cover and chill at least 1 hour. (Can be made 1 day ahead; keep chilled). Prepare grill (medium-high heat). Whisk ¼ cup extra-virgin olive oil, vinegar, and mustard in small bowl to blend. Season dressing with salt and freshly ground black pepper. Slightly overlap tomato slices on large platter. Drizzle with dressing; sprinkle with half of olives. Place wrapped cheese rounds on grill, seam side down. Grill until cheese softens and leaves begin to char, about 2 minutes per side. Arrange cheeses atop tomatoes. Sprinkle with remaining olives. Brush bread slices with remaining thyme oil. Grill bread until beginning to brown, turning occasionally, about 5 minutes. Cut toasts diagonally in half. Serve cheese, passing toasts separately. Yield: 12

Cucumber Boats with Caviar

2 med cucumbers, unpeeled
salt
2 tablespoons sour cream
1 (8 oz) package cream cheese, room temperature
¾ teaspoon onion powder
¼ teaspoon Tabasco
2 ounce red caviar
parsley sprigs

Halve cucumbers lengthwise and scoop out the seeds. Sprinkle insides of halves with salt and invert on paper towels to drain for several hours. Dry very well. In medium bowl mix cream cheese, onion powder, Tabasco and sour cream until well blended. Gently stir in ¾ of caviar. Spoon or pipe mixture through a pastry tube into the cucumbers, mounding slightly. May be refrigerated for up to 5 hours. Before serving, slice stuffed cucumbers crosswise into ¾ inch slices. Garnish each slice with remaining caviar and tiny sprigs of parsley.

Hummus

2 cloves garlic
½ cup tahini (sesame seed paste)
¼ cup water
3 tablespoons olive oil
½ teaspoon cumin
1 teaspoon coriander
¼ teaspoon cayenne
6 tablespoons lemon juice
1 (19 oz) can chick peas, drained
salt
freshly ground black pepper

Chop garlic in food processor until fine. Add tahini, water, olive oil lemon juice, blending until smooth. Add remaining ingredients and process until pureed. Add salt and pepper. If mixture is too thick, add additional water. Spread in a flat plate and garnish with parsley. Serve with pita chips.
Note: I omit tahini to reduce the fat and calories!

Sally West's Croustades

1 loaf thin white loaf bread
butter

Cut thin bread into rounds with a biscuit cutter; butter rounds on one side with a pastry brush; then, press them buttered side down into a mini-muffin tin. Bake at 325° until they are crispy (15 minutes in my oven).
*Sally kept these in a tall glass canister and they remain fresh for weeks. Leftovers can be frozen and quickly refreshed in oven before serving.
**You can use same technique and make larger cups or patty shells to serve an entrée for lunch or dinner. I much prefer these to packaged shells. Rather than serve "dips", I like to put a dollop of any tasty dip in these. Often, I freeze left over Rockefeller sauce, thaw it, heat it, place a dollop in a croustade and have instant hot h'ordeuvres.

Basil Pesto Cheesecake

1 ½ teaspoons butter
¼ cup fine breadcrumbs, lightly toasted
¼ cup grated parmesan cheese
8 oz grated parmesan cheese
2 ½ cups fresh basil
¼ cup parsley sprigs, steamed
¼ cup olive oil
½ teaspoon salt
1 clove garlic, minced
16 ounces fresh whole milk ricotta cheese (room temperature)
2 (8 oz) packages cream cheese
4 eggs
¼ cup pine nuts, lightly toasted
basil leaves for garnish

Butter bottom and sides of a 9-inch spring form pan. Combine breadcrumbs and ¼ cup Parmesan cheese. Sprinkle mixture into pan, turning to coat completely. Refrigerate. Combine basil and next four ingredients in blender or food processor and process until a smooth paste forms (about two minutes), stopping occasionally to scrape down sides. Transfer mixture to a large bowl. Combine ricotta cheese, cream cheese and Parmesan cheese in blender or food processor and mix until smooth (about two minutes). Mix in eggs. Pour basil mixture back into processor with cheese mixture and process together until combined. Pour into prepared pan. Sprinkle top with pine nuts. Place pan on a baking sheet. Bake at 325° for 1 ¼ hours. Turn oven off and cool cheesecake in oven about one hour with door ajar. Transfer to a wire rack. Remove sides from spring form pan. Garnish with basil leaves and serve at room temperature with crackers.
Yield: 15 to 20 servings Contributor: Maria Rosso

My Favorite Cheese Ball

1 pound Wisconsin cheddar
1 large package cream cheese
½ onion-finely chopped
1 tablespoon Worcestershire sauce
1 small jar stuffed olives-chopped
1 teaspoon chili powder
1 cup chopped pecans
1 tablespoon chopped parsley
dash cayenne pepper
1 can paprika
1 can chili powder

Mix cheeses. Next add all ingredients except the cans of paprika and chili powder. Let stand for 20 minutes. Mix the chili and paprika. Shape cheese mixture into balls (approximately 3 inches in diameter or larger, if preferred) and roll in the mixed chili and paprika.
Note: Freezes well. I like to keep small balls in freezer for emergencies. Can be thawed, VERY CAREFULLY, in microwave.
Source: Med School days-Jim Stewart

Oyster and Artichoke Ramekin

3 large artichokes
1 teaspoon salt
4 tablespoons butter
18 large raw oysters with liquor
2 tablespoons flour
1 tablespoon minced parsley
6 large mushrooms, sliced
2 tablespoons minced onion
pepper
salt

Cook artichokes, covered, in salted water for 45 minutes or until bottom tender but firm. Drain and allow cooling. Remove bottoms and cut into cubes. Scrape leaves, set aside. In heavy cold skillet, lightly brown flour and set aside. In another heavy skillet, sauté onion and mushrooms in butter until lightly browned. Remove from heat. Brown flour and mix with parsley. Slowly pour in oyster liquor and simmer 10 minutes. Season to taste. Drop oysters into hot mixture and allow edges to curl. Remove from heat and keep warm. Place artichokes and oysters in six ramekins, dividing equally. Pour oyster and mushroom mixture over and bake in 350° oven for 10 to 15 minutes. Yield: 6 servings

Oysters And Smithfield Ham

2 ¼ cups traditional béchamel sauce
¼ cup ham, diced
½ teaspoon Worcestershire
2 tablespoons dry white wine
1 pint oysters
1 large egg yolk, lightly

Combine béchamel with Worcestershire and keep warm. Cook oysters until edges curl. Add oysters and ham to sauce.
Stir in wine and egg yolk. Serve over toast or with cornbread sticks.

To prepare traditional béchamel sauce:
½ cup all purpose flour
4 tablespoons butter
½ onion, minced
4 cups milk
¼ teaspoon white pepper
¼ teaspoon nutmeg
¼ teaspoon salt
¼ pound veal, chopped
1 sprig thyme

Cook flour 2-3 minutes before whisking in melted butter. Sauté onion until golden and add to flour mixture. Heat milk and add, stirring continuously until it is smooth. Sauté ¼ lb veal in 2 tablespoons butter over very low heat. Season the veal with sprig of thyme or a tiny pinch of leaves. Add a pinch of white pepper and freshly grated nutmeg. Cook the veal for 5 minutes, stirring it frequently to prevent it from browning and stir it into the sauce. Cook the sauce in the top of a double boiler over hot water stirring from time to time until thickened. Strain through fine sieve and dot with bits of butter; they will melt and prevent a film from forming. Makes about one quart.

Cheese Olive Balls

¼ pound NY sharp cheddar
½ teaspoon salt
½ stick butter
½ teaspoon cayenne
1 cup flour
¼ teaspoon paprika
1 jar stuffed olives, drained

Grate cheese. Add butter, flour, salt, cayenne and paprika. Process until well mixed. Roll in palms of hands and flatten (small marble size) just enough dough to cover olive. Have olives well drained (colander and paper towels). Bake 15 minutes at 400°. These freeze well. To prepare for freezer and later use, place unbaked on a cookie sheet and freeze. You can then rake the balls into plastic bags for freezer storage. After freezing, thaw slightly and bake as directed above.

Goat Cheese and Sun-Dried Tomato Tartines

12 (½ inch thick) baguette slices
3 ½ tablespoons extra-virgin olive oil
1 medium tomato, peeled, seeded, and cut into ¼ inch dice
2 tablespoons julienned soft sun-dried tomatoes (packed in oil)
1 tablespoon torn fresh basil
1 teaspoon sherry vinegar
2 tablespoons bottled black olive tapenade
8 ounce soft mild goat cheese log cut crosswise into ½ inch thick slices
garnish: torn fresh basil leaves

Preheat oven to 350°. Brush 1 side of baguette slices with 2 tablespoons oil and arrange oiled sides up, on a baking sheet. Toast bread in middle of oven until golden on top, about 7 minutes, and then transfer to a rack to cool. Leave oven on. Rinse sun dried tomatoes in hot water, drain and pat dry, before dicing them. Stir together fresh and sun dried tomatoes, basil, vinegar, and ½ tablespoon oil. Spread each toast with tapenade and top with a slice of goat cheese and a rounded teaspoon of tomato mixture. Arrange tartines on a baking sheet, then season with salt and pepper and drizzle with ½ tablespoon oil. Bake tartines in middle of oven until cheese is softened, about 5 minutes. Transfer to a platter and drizzle with remaining ½ tablespoon oil.
Note: Toasts may be made 2 days ahead, cooled completely, and kept in airtight container at room temperature. Tomato mixture may be made 1 day ahead and chilled, covered.

Mushrooms Stuffed with Spinach and Oysters

1 pint oysters
3 cloves garlic, chopped
1 package spinach, chopped
1 small can mushrooms, undrained
¼ cup white wine
dash cayenne
freshly ground black pepper
1 teaspoon Worcestershire
dash Tabasco
salt to taste
24 medium sized fresh mushroom caps

Heat oyster liquor in medium sized iron skillet. Add oysters and cook until edges curl. Remove oysters, chop and set aside. Process chopped garlic and spinach and add to oyster liquor. Let simmer on low heat. Add small can of mushrooms with their liquid and the wine. Season with Worcestershire, Tabasco, salt, freshly ground black pepper a cayenne. Stuff mushroom caps and bake in 350° oven. Yield: 12

Brandied Bleu Cheese

1 (8 oz) package cream cheese
2 (4 oz) packages bleu cheese-crumbled
⅓ cup brandy
dash nutmeg

Whip ingredients together. Serve on cocktail wafers.

Dilled Shrimp

1 ½ cups Hellman's low fat mayonnaise
1 large red onion, thinly sliced
⅓ cup fresh lemon juice or to taste
2 tablespoons dried dill
¼ teaspoon salt
2 lbs medium shrimp, cook and peel
¼ cup sugar
½ cup sour cream

Mix all ingredients stir and refrigerate overnight. Stir once before servings.
Note: Good dish for a cocktail buffet. I serve it in a shell server with cocktail pics or 6 inch bamboo skewers on the side.

Chafing Dish Oysters

1 quart oysters, undrained
¼ cup butter
1 (8 oz) package cream cheese, softened
6 tablespoons dry white wine
¼ teaspoon cayenne
¼ teaspoon salt
6 drops Tabasco
½ teaspoon anchovy paste
½ teaspoon paprika
3 tablespoons scallions, chopped
parsley, chopped
4 dozen patty shells or croustades (*see recipe page 10)

Place undrained oysters in saucepan. Cook over medium heat for 2 minutes or until edges curl. Combine butter and cream cheese in a medium saucepan. Place over low heat. When melted, add wine and whisk. Stir in scallions, paprika, anchovy paste, cayenne, salt and Tabasco. Bring to a boil over high heat, stirring constantly. Gently fold in coarsely chopped oysters. Put in chafing dish. Garnish with parsley.

Jay Watkins' Eggplant Sticks

1 eggplant
1 cup salt
1 gallon water
2 cups buttermilk
1 egg
peanut oil-for frying
1 cup flour
1 handful corn meal

Prepare brine, mixing 1 cup salt per gallon of water. Peel eggplant and cut into sticks (approximately ½ inch x 4 inches). Soak sticks in brine for several hours or overnight. Drain sticks and pat dry on paper towels. Heat peanut oil to 350°. Beat egg into buttermilk. Mix flour and meal and place in shallow bowl. Dip sticks in buttermilk mixture, then roll in flour and meal mixture, shaking off excess. Cook until browned at 350° peanut oil. Drain on paper towels and serve immediately.
Note: Created, prepared and served by Jay on their Point Clear wharf the 4th of July !!

Lamb on Skewers with Mint

4 pounds lean lamb, cut into bite size cubes
1 tablespoon salt
freshly ground pepper to taste
½ cup olive oil
1 teaspoon thyme
2 lemons-juiced

Mix ingredients and marinate lamb overnight in a glass bowl. Put 3 Lamb cubes on individual 6 inch bamboo skewers. Grill lightly. Cover skewers with foil if they begin to burn.
Serve with mint sauce or mint chutney. Serves 20-30.

Mushroom Turnovers

Pastry:
1 cup butter, softened
1 (8 oz) package cream cheese
½ teaspoon salt
2 cups flour

Filling:
½ cup chopped onion
½ pound mushrooms chop fine
2 tablespoons butter
2 teaspoon flour
½ cup sour cream
dash ground nutmeg
dash freshly ground pepper
½ teaspoon salt
1 teaspoon lemon juice
1 teaspoon dill weed
2 teaspoon milk
1 egg yolk

To make pastry:
Mix butter, cream cheese, salt and flour to form soft dough. Chill overnight.

To prepare filling:
Sauté onion and mushrooms in butter. Add flour and mix. Gradually add sour cream, salt, freshly ground black pepper, nutmeg, lemon juice and dill weed.

Assembly and baking: Break off portion of dough (keeping remainder chilled until ready to roll) and roll dough thin on a floured surface. Cut with a 2 inch cookie cutter and put ½ teaspoon mushroom filling in center of circle, fold over and crimp with tines of fork. When ready to cook, brush tops with egg yolk beaten with milk. Bake at 350° for 15 minutes.

Note: The uncooked and assembled pastries may be frozen on a cookie sheet and placed in a freezer bag for later use.

Mushroom Filling for Tartlets

½ pound mushrooms chopped
1 clove garlic, pressed
3 tablespoons butter
2 tablespoons cognac
½ cup sour cream

Make tartlet shells and bake (*see pate brisee recipe page 327 and use for shells). Sauté mushrooms and garlic in butter until tender. Add cognac, cook until absorbed. Remove from heat, add sour cream. Fill tartlet shells and heat before servings.

Note: Can make shells and filling ahead, freezing both, and assembling before serving. Serves 24.

Portobello Pizza

1 portobello mushroom
1 tablespoon olive oil
¼ cup sun dried tomatoes with herbs
¼ cup Kalamata olives, chopped
¼ cup crumbled feta cheese
chopped fresh basil

Clean mushroom, remove and chop stem (reserve). Heat oil in large skillet over medium heat. Sear portobello 2 minutes on each side. Cook diced stem until golden, stir in tomatoes and olives. Stuff mushroom with mixture and top with feta. Broil 2 to 3 minutes. Sprinkle tops with finely chopped basil.

Oysters Rockefeller

1 pint oysters
6 tablespoons butter
salt to taste
1 package fresh spinach, minced
freshly ground black pepper
dash cayenne
½ bunch parsley, minced
¼ cup finely chopped watercress
3 stalks celery, minced
3 tablespoons fine dry bread crumbs
¼ cup absinthe or pernod
dash of Tabasco

Melt butter in saucepan. Stir in all ingredients, except oysters. Cook over low heat, stirring frequently, for 15 minutes. Puree in blender or food processor. Place oysters in empty shell or ramekin and bake at 450° until edges of oyster curl (about 10 minutes). Remove from oven, pour off excess liquid, and top oysters with sauce. Return to oven and cook 5 to 10 minutes until slightly brown and bubbly on top. Serve immediately.

The sauce can be made ahead and frozen. I use it in croustades as an appetizer. Also, for almost instant Oysters Rockefeller, I fill plastic ice cube trays with this sauce and keep them in my freezer. I keep a bag of cleaned oyster shells hanging in a bag in my pantry and when ready to serve, I place an oyster in each shell, pop out a cube of partially thawed Rockefeller sauce, put it on top of the oyster, heat for about 10 minutes in a 375° oven.

Note: If frozen, freshen with a few drops of Pernod.

Pesto Torte

4 ounces goat cheese
¾ cup freshly grated parmesan cheese
12 ounces cream cheese, softened
½ cup butter, softened
½ cup sour cream
¾ cup minced sundried tomatoes, in oil
¾ cup pesto sauce
fresh basil leaves for garnish

Place cheeses, butter and sour cream in the bowl of a food processor and process until smooth, about 1 minute. Spritz a 6 cup mold or loaf pan with cooking spray line with plastic and lightly spritz again. Spread the minced tomatoes on the bottom of the plastic-lined mold. Spread ⅓ of the cheese mixture over the tomatoes, followed by ½ of the pesto. Repeat layers, ending with cheese. Cover loosely with plastic wrap and refrigerate for at least 3 hours. (Can be kept in the refrigerator for up to two weeks or frozen.) To unmold, remove plastic wrap from the top, turn the mold upside down on serving platter, and carefully pull off the remaining wrap. Garnish with fresh basil, Serve with simple crackers or crusty bread rounds. This recipe will make three 6 inch tortes or you can make a single large torte.

Pasta Shells with Chicken Salad

1 chicken, cooked, deboned and cut into bite size pieces
2 carrots
1 onion
6 sprigs parsley
¼ teaspoon freshly ground pepper
1 teaspoon salt
1 teaspoon celery salt
1 ½ cups diced celery
lemon juice to taste
olives for garnish
artichoke hearts for garnish
cherry tomatoes for garnish
fresh basil or parsley for garnish
40 conchiglie shells, cooked al dente
1 bottle BRS lemon vinaigrette (*see recipe page 84)

Cook pasta shells the day before in salted water with some olive oil. Drain shells and put in zip lock bag with the bottle of vinaigrette to marinate overnight before stuffing. Cook chicken in water seasoned with the carrots, onion and 6 sprigs parsley. Let chicken cool in its own broth before skinning, deboning and cutting into large bite size pieces. Mix chicken with celery, mayonnaise, salt, freshly ground black pepper, celery salt and lemon juice. Stuff shells with the chicken salad and garnish with olives, cherry tomatoes, artichoke hearts, etc.
Note: Good to take to covered dish party in summer along with a basket of mini-muffins.

Tzatziki

½ English cucumber, peeled, drained and grated
1 (16 oz) carton Greek yogurt, (or regular plain yogurt strained through
        cheese cloth)
2 to 10 cloves garlic chopped
2 teaspoons lemon juice
1 tablespoon olive oil

Prepare all ingredients in advance. Combine oil and lemon juice in a medium mixing bowl. Fold the yogurt in slowly, making sure it mixes completely with the oil. Add the garlic, according to taste, and the cucumber. Stir until evenly distributed. Garnish with a bit of green cucumber peel and serve well chilled. This keeps for several days in refrigerator; however, you will need to drain off any water and stir each time before serving. Yield: about 2 ½ cups

Nibbles for the Starved Man

Meals last longer and taste better when you nibble

Having been starved, you savor every bite

With easy deglutition, your nourishment enters a dark receptive, magic place

That holds it lovingly and finally lets it go

Lets it go to rest and prepare for the next nibble

Hopefully, the starved man will enjoy his food

And beg for another bite…..

Beverages

Cider Wassail Bowl

1 large tart apple (granny smith), unpeeled, cored, and sliced ¼ inch thick
1 teaspoon lemon juice
5 tablespoons dark brown sugar
1 tablespoon unsalted butter
1 quart apple cider
1 tablespoon grated lemon zest
1 tablespoons grated orange zest
6 allspice berries
5 cardamom pods
1 stick cinnamon, break in half
6 whole cloves
½ cup dark rum
½ cup apple brandy
1 can light ale

Toss apple slices in lemon juice. Arrange them in a shallow baking pan in a single layer. Sprinkle with 1 tablespoon of the brown sugar. Dot with butter. Bake For 20 minutes and let cool slightly. Bring the cider, lemon, orange zest, and the remaining brown sugar to a boil over high heat, stirring to dissolve the sugar. Tie the cardamom, cinnamon and cloves in cheesecloth and add to the cider mixture. Cover and simmer over low heat for 20 minutes. Add the rum, brandy and ale. Remove from heat and discard the spice bag. Pour the cider into a punch bowl. Garnish with the apple slices. Sprinkle with nutmeg.

Holiday Kitchen Wassail

2 quarts apple cider
1 teaspoon allspice berries
1 pint cranberry juice
1 small orange, studded with cloves
¾ cup sugar
1 teaspoon bitters
1 cup rum
2 sticks cinnamon

Put all ingredients in a crockpot. Cover and cook on high for 1 hour, then on low for 4 to 8 hours.

Note: Each holiday season, I prepare this in a crockpot or slow cooker and keep it in my kitchen. It not only provides a delightful aroma, but, is readily available to enjoy sipping throughout the day. With it, you are always ready for holiday visitors!

Easy Egg Nog

½ quart eggnog ice cream
nutmeg
1 pint half and half
½ quart dark rum

Mix all ingredients and serve in a punch bowl.
Contributor: Marynell Perkins

Health Drink

½ carrot, washed
⅛ lemon, with peel
1 cantaloupe, without seeds, with peel
1/8 cabbage, raw
½ orange, peeled with white left on
½ apple, with seed and unpeeled
¾ cup pineapple juice, unsweetened
2 cups ice
2 tablespoons honey
½ banana, peeled

The cantaloupe should be scrubbed well, since the peel is included. Put all ingredients in heavy duty blender and blend. Yield: 4 servings

Bubbling Holiday Punch (Cold Duck)

1 (10 oz) pkg frozen strawberries, thawed
2 limes, thinly sliced
water
2 cups light rum
2 (6 oz) cans frozen daiquiri concentrate
⅗ Cold Duck, chilled

For ice ring, pour water into a ring mold to depth of 1 inch and freeze. Arrange strawberries and lime slices around mold over ice. Add enough water to anchor fruit to ice. Freeze. Fill mold with water, freeze mold. To serve, combine rum and daiquiri mix in punch bowl. Carefully add ice ring. Pour in chilled Cold Duck.

Almost a Rubaiyat Night

My bread is baked
My jug is filled
Where art thou?

Soups

Fresh Cold Corn Chowder

1 cup fresh corn kernels (use Silver Queen corn, if available)
½ cup scallions, chopped
1 quart buttermilk
salt to taste
juice of ½ lime
lime zest

Boil corn 5 minutes, cool, then cut kernels from cob. Chop scallions. Mix all ingredients and chill for at least 2 hours before serving.

Chilled Avocado Soup
with Caviar

3 avocados
3 cups chicken broth
1 cup plain yogurt
3 tablespoons fresh lime juice
freshly ground black pepper to taste
2 tablespoons caviar

Peel, pit, and coarsely chop the avocados. Place in food processor and puree. With the motor running add the broth in a stream. Add 1 cup yogurt and process the mixture until it is smooth. Blend in the lime juice, salt and freshly ground black pepper to taste, transfer the soup to a bowl, cover with plastic wrap and chill it for 2 hours, or until it is cold. Ladle the soup into chilled bowls, swirl in the additional yogurt, decoratively, and top each serving with a spoon of caviar. Makes about 6 cups. Yield: 4 servings

Gazpacho

1 white onion
1 ½ cucumbers, peeled
2 green bell peppers
12 tomatoes, peeled
6 cloves garlic
1 cup tomato juice
¼ cup light olive oil
1 ½ tablespoons Creole seasoning
1 ½ tablespoons sea salt
1 teaspoon cumin

Process onion, transfer from work bowl to a large bowl. Repeat with cucumbers, then the green peppers, adding to large bowl as processed. Peel tomatoes by first dipping in hot water to loosen skins. Process all but one of the tomatoes and add to the other vegetables. With processor on, add garlic cloves through tube to process. Next add the last tomato and process well. Then pour in tomato juice, olive oil, Creole seasoning, cumin, and salt. Continue processing until a smooth liquid is formed. Add to other ingredients and refrigerate.
*Bloody Mary mix is a good extender!

Spicy Cucumber-Avocado Soup

½ firm, ripe California avocado
1 ¾ English cucumbers (cut into ½ inch pieces)
1 cup (8 oz) plain low-fat yogurt
3 tablespoons chopped fresh chives
1 teaspoon fresh lime juice
1 teaspoon salt, or to taste
½ teaspoon chopped fresh jalapeño chili, without seeds
1 cup small ice cubes
 Garnish with chopped parsley and chives

Peel and pit avocado. Blend all ingredients in a blender until very smooth, about one minute. Ladle into chilled bowls.
Yield: 6 servings

Artichoke-Oyster Soup

¼ pound butter
2 bunches green onions, chopped
3 ribs celery, chopped
3 cloves garlic, pressed
3 tablespoons flour
1 ½ quarts chicken stock
2 (14 oz) cans artichoke hearts, drained and quartered, saving liquor
1 teaspoon red pepper flakes
1 teaspoon salt
1 tablespoon Worcestershire
1 teaspoon anise seeds
1 quart oysters, drained and chopped
1 cup evaporated milk

Melt butter in heavy 4-quart pot. Sauté onions, celery, and garlic until brown. Lightly brown flour, slowly stir in stock (heated), whisking until smooth. Add chopped artichokes and seasonings. Cover and simmer 1 hour. Next, add chopped oysters (oysters can be chopped by placing in processor and pulsing only twice). Simmer 10 minutes, do not boil. Stir in milk. Refrigerate at least 8 hours, or up to 3 days. Before serving reheat gently (do not boil) and serve. Freezes well.

Cream of Asparagus with Crayfish

2 pounds fresh asparagus, peeled and cut into pieces
3 cups chicken broth
2 shallots, finely chopped
¼ cup butter
5 tablespoons flour
3 cups half and half
1 teaspoon curry powder
salt to taste
2 tablespoons sherry
1 cup crayfish tails

Place asparagus in large saucepan with broth and shallots and cook until tender. Remove 8 asparagus tips and set aside for garnish. Blend remaining asparagus in food processor until smooth. Melt butter, add flour and cook for three minutes, stirring constantly. Add asparagus puree and half and half. Stir until blended. Add seasonings and sherry and simmer 10 minutes. Add crayfish and simmer 5 minutes or until crayfish heated through. Garnish with extra crayfish, asparagus spears, or croutons cut into fish shapes. Yield: 8 servings

Garides Me Feta
(Shrimp Soup)

½ cup minced onion
1 ½ tablespoon butter
1 ½ tablespoons olive oil
½ cup dry white wine
4 med ripe tomatoes, seeded and chopped
1 clove garlic, minced
1 teaspoon salt
¼ teaspoon freshly ground pepper
¼ teaspoon oregano
1 pound shrimp (raw), peeled and deveined
4 ounces feta cheese, crumbled
¼ cup chopped fresh parsley

In a heavy skillet, sauté onion in butter and oil until soft. Add wine, tomatoes, garlic, salt, pepper, and oregano. Bring to a boil, lower the heat medium, and simmer until sauce is slightly thickened. Stir in cheese and simmer for 10 to 15 minutes. Adjust seasonings. Just before serving, add shrimp to hot sauce and cook for 4-5 minutes or until shrimp turn pink. Do not overcook. Garnish with parsley and serve immediately in large bowls with crusty French bread. Yield: 4 servings

Sophia Clikas' Tomato-Oyster Soup

1 medium onion, slivered
¾ cup celery, with leaves
4 sprigs parsley
4 tablespoons oil
1 dash oregano
2 large cans tomatoes
1 can Rotel tomatoes
1 ½ cloves garlic, slivered
1 ¾ teaspoon salt
¼ teaspoon freshly ground black pepper
2 cups oyster liquor
1 squirt tomato paste
1 cup water
1 pint oysters

Sauté onion, celery, and parsley in 4 tablespoons vegetable oil. Cook until transparent. Add oregano, tomatoes, garlic, salt, and freshly ground black pepper. Cook 2 to 3 minutes. Add oyster liquor, water and tomato paste and simmer 20 to 30 minutes. At this point, base may be frozen. Thaw and add oysters and bring to a boil once or twice, just until oyster edges curl.

BRS Favorite Seafood Gumbo

Stock:

3 quarts water

2 dozen boiled blue crabs

3 pounds raw shrimp in shells with heads on

1 carrot

1 onion, quartered

½ cup celery, coarsely chop

Put water in large stock pot. Pull shells off of crabs, adding shells to water. Discard inedible spongy fibers, break crabs in half and put aside. Peel shrimp, adding shells and heads to pot. Set shrimp aside. Add carrot, onion and celery to pot. Cover and simmer 2 hours. Strain and return stock to pot.

**Can substitute Knorr's Fish Bouillon cubes or clam juice and chicken broth to make a quick stock.

Gumbo:

3 cloves garlic, chopped

3 onions, chopped

1 ½ cups celery, chopped

3 lbs okra, cut into 1/4 inch rounds

1 tablespoons bacon grease

2 tablespoons flour

1 bell pepper, chopped

1 (16 oz) can tomatoes

8 whole allspice

1 teaspoon thyme

1 teaspoon basil

1 can Rotel tomatoes

1 quart chicken broth
3 quarts water or stock
½ cup diced ham or sausage
½ bottle Bovril or Vegemite
4 bay leaves
freshly ground black pepper to taste
salad oil
2 tablespoons Worcestershire
1 teaspoon Tabasco
1 (4 oz) can tomato paste
2 tablespoons soy sauce
1 teaspoon celery seed
2 tablespoons Tony Cachere's Seasoning
½ cup lemon juice
cooked rice

To make gumbo, sauté the garlic, onion, celery, and green pepper in 1/4 cup oil. Cook okra separately in ¾ cup oil for 40 to 50 minutes until soft ropy texture is gone. Stir often. In separate pan make a roux with bacon grease and flour by cooking over low heat, stirring often until brown. (I substitute flour browned without bacon grease or Tony Cachere's Roux). Add tomatoes (broken into pieces) to roux and cook into a paste. Add allspice thyme, basil and bay leaves. Cook 5 to 10 minutes. Add sauté mixture, Rotel tomatoes, other seasonings and okra to stock. Gradually add seasoned roux mixture to stock. Simmer for 1 ½ to 2 hours. Add seafood and parsley. Season with additional salt, pepper, Tabasco, Worcestershire, lemon juice, and Tony Cachere's Famous Creole Seasoning, if needed. Cook an additional ½ hour. Serve over rice Freezes well.
*May need more roux than original recipe makes.
Yield: 6 servings

Redfish Court Bouillon

½ cup flour
¼ cup oil
2 cups chopped onion
1 cup chopped celery
1 cup chopped bell pepper
2 bay leaves
¼ teaspoon thyme
¼ teaspoon sweet basil
¼ teaspoon dill
½ cup mushrooms
4 tablespoons tomato paste
4 cloves chopped garlic
1 teaspoon whole allspice
4 cups water
2 tablespoons lemon juice
salt to taste
cayenne to taste
1 tablespoon Worcestershire
2 tablespoons chopped parsley
3 lbs fish fillets
½ cup white wine

In heavy pot, cook oil and flour until golden brown. Add onions, celery, bell peppers; sauté until soft. Add all ingredients except parsley, fish, and wine. Blend well and simmer over medium heat approximately half an hour. Cut fish into cubes; add to sauce. Stir wine and parsley. Season to taste. Add water to retain volume. Yield: 6 servings

Turkey Bone Gumbo

1 turkey carcass (include meat, skin, and bones)
5 cloves garlic
½ bunch carrots
2 onions, halved
tops from bunch of celery
parsley
2 teaspoons Spice Islands chicken stock base
1½ teaspoons freshly ground pepper
salt to taste
3 bay leaves
thyme
lemon pepper marinade
garlic salt
2 large cans (18 oz) tomatoes
2 small cans tomato sauce
1 bag frozen white shoe-peg corn
1 bag frozen butter beans
1 large package wide noodles

Remove any visible fat from turkey carcass, then place it in a large 8 to 10 quart pot and cover with water. Add garlic, onions, celery tops, parsley, chicken stock, freshly ground black pepper and bay leaves. Simmer 6 or 7 hours. Remove bones and vegetables, strain broth and reserve the broth. Remove meat from bones, discarding bones and reserving all meat. Pick out the carrots and discard remainder of vegetables. Mash carrots. To about 4 quarts of the reserved broth, add tomatoes, tomato sauce, corn, butterbeans, thyme, mashed carrots, the turkey meat and remaining seasonings. Simmer 45 minutes. Add noodles the last 15 minutes. (I do not add the noodles, to cut the calories; however, if you prefer you can add them.)

*Should you have less than 4 qts of broth, use supplemental chicken broth. Should you have extra broth, save it for other uses.
Yield: 20 servings

My Black Bean Soup

2 pounds black beans
½ pound ham hocks or ham bone
2 large onions, quartered
4 stalks celery, outside and untrimmed
3 cloves garlic, sliced
6 bay leaves
6 whole allspice
lemon slices
2 tablespoons Worcestershire
2 tablespoons lemon juice
6 tablespoons basil vinegar
3 quarts water
salt to taste
½ cup dry sherry
cloves
onions, chopped
rice

Soak beans overnight in cold water, if time permits. Drain beans. Add quartered onions, celery, garlic, bay leaves, allspice, Worcestershire, lemon juice, vinegar, and water to beans in heavy pot. Bring to a boil, reduce heat and simmer, covered, for 4 hours or until beans are tender. Season with salt and pepper to taste (I use approximately 1 ½ teaspoons of salt and ½ teaspoon of pepper). Remove ham, onions, and celery. Force at least ½ of beans through sieve. Return sieved beans to pot. Return bean skins to pot, also. At this point, season to taste with salt. Cook another 30 minutes. Add sherry a few minutes before serving. Serve with side dishes of rice and chopped onion.

Storing Love

A squirrel gathers nuts for the winter
Why shouldn't we each day
Gather bits of love and tuck them away
Save them for cold and empty days?

I gathered nuts today
An unexpected call from an old friend
Homemade rolls that tasted as those of childhood
Warm letters to and from old friends

These give me warm feelings
They are love
I go back and eat them during my winter moments.

Salads & Salad Dressings

Cranberry and Orange Salad Mold

1 (3 oz) package cherry Jello
1 cup hot water
¾ cup sugar
2 tablespoons lemon juice
1 tablespoon gelatin
1 cup pineapple juice
1 cup crushed pineapple, drained
1 cup chopped pecans
2 cups raw cranberries, ground
2 whole oranges

Dissolve cherry Jello in hot water. Add sugar and lemon juice. Soak gelatin in pineapple juice and dissolve over hot water. Add to cherry gelatin. When gelatin begins to thicken, add other ingredients and pour into mold. Chill until well set. Unmold and serve.

Crab Meat Mousse

1 tablespoon gelatin
3 tablespoons cold water
¼ cup mayonnaise
2 tablespoons lime juice
2 tablespoons lemon juice
1 tablespoon parsley, chopped
¾ cup heavy cream, whipped
limes, sliced thin
1 tablespoon prepared mustard
salt to taste
freshly ground pepper
2 cups crab meat, flaked
2 avocados, mashed with lime juice
1 tablespoon chives

Soften gelatin in cold water and dissolve it over hot water. Mix the gelatin with mayonnaise, lime and lemon juice, parsley, chives, and mustard. Add salt and freshly ground black pepper to taste. Fold in crab meat and whipped cream. Pour into buttered ring mold and chill. Unmold on a chilled platter. Garnish with thin slices of lime. Fill center with avocado and sprinkle with fresh chives.

Crabmeat Mousse

Avocado and Grapefruit Salad

1 ½ packages plain gelatin
½ cup cold water
1 ½ cups avocado, mashed
1 teaspoon horseradish
2 tablespoons lemon juice
dash Tabasco
2 cups buttermilk
½ cup mayonnaise
1 ½ teaspoon salt
dash celery salt
1 tablespoon onion, grated
drop of green food coloring
grapefruit sections
avocado slices
lettuce

Soften gelatin in cold water; dissolve over hot water. Cool slightly, then add to seeded and mashed avocado and mix well. Add all other ingredients, except grapefruit sections and avocado slices. Pour into oiled 8 cup ring mold and chill until firm. Unmold on salad greens and fill center with grapefruit sections and avocado slices.

Avocado and Grapefruit Salad

BRS Avocado-Caper-Celery Salad

1 avocado, sliced
2 leaves romaine
1 stalk celery, diced
2 slices bacon, crumbled
2 teaspoon capers, drained
BRS Lemon Vinaigrette (*see recipe page 84)

Marinade avocado and celery bits in BRS vinaigrette for 30 minutes or more. Drain and place on a lettuce bed. Sprinkle with capers and bacon bits. Serve additional vinaigrette on side. Serves: 2

Congealed Apricot Ring with Fresh Fruit

3 ½ packages apricot Jello
6 cups orange juice
1(8 oz) package cream cheese
½ cup sour cream
¼ cup confectioner's sugar
fresh fruits: honeydew, cantaloupe, grapes, pineapple and/or kiwi
mint for garnish

Chill 4 cups of juice in freezer. Dissolve Jello in 2 cups of heated juice. Cool slightly and add 2 cups of chilled juice. Pour into ring mold and chill until set. Unmold on chilled tray. Surround with fresh fruit. Garnish with fresh mint. Serve with side dish of dressing. To prepare dressing, mix cream cheese, sour cream, sugar, and 2 cups of chilled juice. Process until smooth and chill.

*When time allows, I prepare congealed salads a day ahead and check early to see if well congealed. If not, dissolve ½ package of additional Jello or gelatin in small amount of liquid and add to unmolded, partially melted mixture. Pour back into the ring mold and try again!

** To unmold congealed salad, I fill my kitchen sink with 2 or 3 inches of hot water. Carefully, lower the mold into the water for a few seconds, remove, place serving plate on top of mold and invert. If your salad does not release immediately, you may need to gently slip the blade of a knife along the edge to release the salad.

Quinoa with Mango and Curried Yogurt

⅓ cup plain yogurt
1 tablespoon fresh lime juice
2 teaspoons curry powder
1 teaspoon fresh ginger, peeled and finely grated
¾ teaspoon salt
¼ teaspoon freshly ground pepper
2 tablespoons vegetable or peanut oil
1 ⅓ cups quinoa (7 ½ oz)
1 pound firm (ripe) mango, peeled, pitted, and cut into ½ inch pieces
1 red bell pepper, cut into ¼ inch dice
1 fresh jalapeño chile, seeded
⅓ cup chopped fresh mint
½ cup salted roasted peanuts, chopped

Whisk together yogurt, lime juice, curry powder, ginger, salt, and freshly ground black pepper in a large bowl. Add oil in a slow stream, whisking until combined. Rinse quinoa in a bowl using 5 changes of water, rubbing grains and letting them settle before pouring off water. Cook quinoa in a 4 to 5 quart pot of boiling salted water 10 minutes. Drain in a large sieve and rinse under cold running water. Set sieve with quinoa over a saucepan containing ½ inches boiling water (sieve should not touch water) and steam quinoa, covered with a kitchen towel and lid, until fluffy and dry, 10 to 12 minutes. Toss quinoa with curried yogurt and remaining ingredients in a large bowl. Serve warm or at room temperature.

Aspic Piquante

2 (3 oz) pkgs lemon Jello
2 cups boiling water
1 (10 oz) can tomatoes
1 (10 oz) can Rotel tomatoes
1 teaspoon celery salt
½ lemon, juiced
½ cup diced celery

Dissolve gelatin in boiling water. Mix tomatoes and buzz in processor. Add celery salt and lemon juice. Refrigerate until slightly thickened. Add chopped celery and pour into 1-½ qt mold or into individual molds.

Cranberry Salad Ring

2 cups fresh cranberries
1 ¼ cups water
1 cup sugar
1 package cherry Jello
1 cup boiling water
¾ cup celery, diced
½ cup pecans, chopped
¼ teaspoon salt
lettuce

Cook cranberries in 1 ¼ cups water until soft. When soft add sugar and cook 5 minutes. Pour boiling mixture over cherry gelatin, stir until dissolved. Chill until partially set, add celery and pecans. Place mixture in oiled rind mold and chill. Unmold on lettuce bed.

Asparagus with Goat Cheese and Walnuts

24 fresh asparagus tips
8 cups strongly flavored greens - Bibb, chicory, or other tender lettuce
12 walnut halves, crumbled and toasted
⅓ pound strongly flavored goat cheese
2 tablespoons walnut oil
2 teaspoons white vinegar

Place the asparagus tips in 2 quarts of salted, boiling water, and cook just until tender (about 3 minutes). Reserve. Wash and dry the greens thoroughly, tear into small pieces. When ready to serve, place the greens in a large bowl. Toss with the asparagus and half of the walnut crumbs. Beat the oil and vinegar in a separate bowl, season to taste and toss with the salad. Arrange the dressed salad on four salad plates, making a symmetrical arrangement of the asparagus tips. Cut the goat cheese into 12 pieces, and divide the pieces among salads. Sprinkle remaining walnut crumbs over the goat cheese pieces. Yield: 4 servings

Avocado Mousse

2 cups avocado
1 teaspoon salt
½ teaspoon white pepper
½ cup mayonnaise
1 tablespoon onion or lemon juice
1 tablespoon gelatin
¼ cup cold water
¾ cup heavy cream, whipped
chopped parsley or Belgian endive

Peel, seed, and mash the avocado. Stir salt, freshly ground black pepper and lemon or onion juice into the mashed avocado. Sprinkle gelatin over ¼ cup cold water and dissolve over hot water. Fold this into mashed avocado. Whip the cream and fold into avocado mixture. Pour into mold. Chill the mousse about 3 hours and unmold it on a chilled platter. Garnish the mousse with chopped parsley and endive leaves.

Tabouleh

2 cups cracked bulgur wheat
¾ cup tomatoes, peel, seed and chop fine
1 ½ cups scallions, chopped
1 cup olive oil
1 cup lemon juice
salt to taste
freshly ground black pepper
garlic, minced (optional)
2 cups parsley, chopped fine
1 cup fresh mint, chopped

Soak the bulgur in water to cover for 2 hours. Drain well and squeeze out any excess moisture. Put in salad bowl and toss in other ingredient with 2 forks.

Chopped mint can be added to tabouleh or leaves used as garnish with tomato wedges.

Cole Slaw

4 cups shredded cabbage
3 green onions, chopped
1 tablespoon mayonnaise
1 teaspoon mustard
¼ teaspoon freshly ground black pepper
1 carrot, shredded

Mix all ingredients and refrigerate. Yield: 8 servings

Fresh Spinach Salad and Dressing

1 ½ lbs fresh spinach
6 sliced bacon, fried crisp
3 eggs, boiled
4 green onions, sliced
½ lb fresh mushrooms
Dressing ingredients:
⅔ cup salad oil
⅓ cup wine vinegar
1 teaspoon salt
¼ teaspoon dry mustard
2 cloves garlic, crushed or sliced
freshly ground pepper
½ teaspoon sugar

Wash spinach well and pat dry. Remove stems and break leaves into bite sized pieces. Break bacon into bits and chop eggs. Toss spinach, bacon, onions and mushrooms lightly.

Salad dressing:
Prepare dressing by combining vinegar, oil, salt, mustard, sugar, garlic and pepper. Mix well. Store in refrigerator.

Cottage Cheese and Beet Salad

1 jar (16-ounce) pickled beet slices
4 hard-boiled eggs, peeled
2 tablespoons plain yogurt
2 tablespoons mayonnaise
2 tablespoons sour cream
salt to taste
¼ tsp white pepper
1 bunch green onions

Place whole hard-boiled eggs in a bowl with the pickled beet slices and their juice and refrigerate for several hours or overnight. Mix the cottage cheese with the yogurt and mayonnaise. Season lightly with salt and white pepper. Trim bulb ends of onions and make vertical slits to splay the onions. When ready to assemble, mound the cottage cheese mixture on an oblong platter. Place beet slices around edge. Halve the pickled eggs and with yolk side down, place them around the edge above the beets. Surround the prepared mound with the onions.

Note: This makes a tasty and festive salad to serve with Easter lamb.

Beet and Cottage Cheese Salad

Incredible Salad

Cranberry Sauce:
1 package fresh cranberries
1 ½ cups brown sugar, light or dark; do not pack
⅓ cup lemonade concentrate
2 tablespoons of orange juice concentrate
½ cup chopped crystallized ginger
½ teaspoon cinnamon
½ teaspoon cardamom
¼ cup rum, any kind

Salad dressing:
¼ cup balsamic vinegar
¼ cup canola oil
¼ cup orange juice concentrate
2 tablespoons lemonade concentrate
1 tablespoon Dijonnaise
1 teaspoon lemon pepper
1 teaspoon mustard powder
½ teaspoon salt
½ cup cranberry sauce (the one just made)

Salad:
10 ounces salad greens, spinach, romaine (need a heavier leaf for this dressing)
1 bunch green onions, chopped
½ cup red grapes, halved
½ cup green grapes, halved
1 tub strawberries, hulled and quartered
1 (11 oz) can Mandarin oranges, drained
Praline Pecans (recipe follows on page 75)

Make the cranberry sauce first, it only takes 5 minutes. Make it by mixing cranberries with sugar and concentrates. Bring to a boil and cook until berries start popping. Toss in ginger and spices. Return to boil and simmer a minute or two. Set aside. (Extra sauce can be used for many other purposes).

Next prepare the salad dressing: Blend all ingredients, which include some of the cranberry sauce, and set dressing aside.

Mix all salad ingredients. Toss the greens, add dressing, and top with praline pecans (a must!).

*If you do not find praline pecans at your favorite Nut House, you can make them by tossing toasted pecans in brown sugar that has been melted to boiling in an iron skillet. Remove nuts with slotted spoon and place on waxed paper to cool before adding to salad.

Cold Rice/Shrimp Salad

1 package Uncle Ben's chicken flavor rice
1-2 green onions and tops, chopped
½ green bell pepper, chopped
12 large stuffed olives, sliced
2 (6 oz) jars marinated artichoke hearts
½ teaspoon curry powder
½ cup mayonnaise, scant
1 pound shrimp, boiled and peeled

Cook rice according to directions and cool. Add onions, pepper, and olives to rice. Drain artichokes and save juice. Combine juice and curry powder with mayonnaise. Pour over rice and sliced artichokes and shrimp and chill. Better done the day before. If chicken flavor rice cannot be obtained, cook 1 cup rice in chicken broth until done. Yield: 4-6 servings

Curried Turkey Salad

2 cups mayonnaise
1 tablespoon Creole mustard
1 tablespoon caraway vinegar
1 tablespoon Worcestershire
1 tablespoon Tabasco
1 tablespoon curry powder
2 teaspoons salt
2 teaspoons freshly ground pepper
4 ribs celery, chopped
½ bunch green onion tops, chopped
2 lbs cooked turkey or chicken, deboned and skinned, coarsely chopped
1 cup red seedless grapes
1 medium yellow onion, chopped

Put all ingredients in a bowl and stir. Yield: Serves 6

Creamy Avocado Mold

1 (3 oz) package lemon Jello
1 cup boiling water
½ cup cold water
1 avocado
¾ cup cheddar cheese, shredded
⅓ cup sour cream
2 tablespoons Sauterne or white wine
1 tablespoons pimento, chopped
¼ teaspoon celery salt

Pour boiling water over gelatin, stir until dissolved. Add cold water and chill until partially set. Add mashed avocado, cheese, sour cream, wine, pimento and celery salt. Turn into 4 cup mold. Chill.
Note: Pretty and tasty for luncheon served with slices of ham rolled around asparagus spears.

Gazpacho Filled Avocado

1 ½ tablespoons finely chopped onion
¼ cup tomato, peeled, seeded, and finely chopped
3 tablespoons cucumber, finely chopped
3 tablespoons green bell pepper, finely chopped
½ teaspoon minced bottled pickled jalapeño
2 teaspoons fresh lemon juice, plus additional for brushing the avocado
        to prevent them turning dark
salt to taste
1 avocado
corn tortilla chips, as an accompaniment

In a small bowl combine the onion, tomato, cucumber, bell pepper, jalapeño, and lemon juice, then salt to taste. Halve and pit the avocado. Brush the avocado halves with additional lemon juice, divide the filling between them, and serve with tortilla chips. Yield: 2 servings

Hot Chicken Salad

2 cups cooked chicken, chopped
1 can cream of celery soup
½ cup chopped pecans
2 cups chopped celery
¾ cup mayonnaise
3 tablespoons minced onion
1 small can sliced mushrooms
3 tablespoons lemon juice
½ teaspoon salt
½ teaspoon freshly ground pepper
½ cup potato chips-crushed

Mix all ingredients except the soup and potato chips. Place in a 2-quart casserole. Pour soup over top without mixing. Top with crushed potato chips and bake at 300° for 30 minutes.

Note: Freezes well (do not add soup or chips before freezing!). Fresh fruit with poppy seed dressing is a good accompaniment.

Wild Rice and Artichoke Salad

3 cups wild rice, cooked and cooled
½ cup quartered artichoke hearts
½ cup pimento, diced
2 tablespoons vinaigrette dressing

Mix all ingredients and serve without chilling.

Old Fashioned Potato Salad

5 medium potatoes, cooked, jackets slipped off, slightly cooled
1 ¼ teaspoons salt
¼ teaspoon freshly ground black pepper
¼ teaspoon celery seed
dash onion salt
5 green onions, sliced
2 tablespoons diced sweet pickle
6 hard boiled eggs, diced
½ cup mayonnaise
2 teaspoons Dijon mustard
Garnish: green pepper, hard boiled eggs, paprika

Boil unpeeled potatoes in water until they can be pierced with a fork (15-20 minutes). Combine diced potatoes with salt and freshly ground black pepper in a large bowl. Combine dressing ingredients and pour over still warm potatoes, mixing thoroughly. Add green onions, sweet pickle and diced eggs; mix thoroughly. Chill.

Picnic Pasta Salad

1 package (16 oz) rotini pasta
1 (8 oz) can tomato sauce
1 cup Italian dressing
1 tablespoon chopped fresh basil leaves or 1 teaspoon dried basil leaves
1 tablespoon chopped fresh oregano leaves or 1 teaspoon dried oregano leaves
1 cup sliced fresh mushrooms
5 Roma (plum) tomatoes, coarsely chopped
1 large cucumber, coarsely chopped
1 medium red onion, chopped
1 can (2 ¼ oz) sliced ripe olives, drained

Cook and drain pasta as directed on package. Rinse with cold water; drain. Mix tomato sauce, dressing, basil, and oregano in large bowl. Add pasta and remaining ingredients; toss. Cover and refrigerate about 2 hours until chilled but no longer than 48 hours. Yield: 12 servings

BRS Lemon Vinaigrette

⅓ cup olive oil
1 teaspoon Dijon mustard
⅔ cup lemon juice
2 cloves garlic, slivered
1 teaspoon salt
½ teaspoon ground black pepper
1 teaspoon balsamic vinegar

Mix and shake all ingredients together. Do not refrigerate.

Homemade Mayonnaise

1 teaspoon. Dijon mustard
2 egg yolks at room temperature
1 tablespoon lemon juice
2 teaspoons wine vinegar
¼ teaspoon salt
2 drops Tabasco
1 cup vegetable oil from a relatively new bottle

Mix the first six ingredients together with a wire whisk in a bowl until the mixture is uniform and beginning to thicken. Add the oil drop by drop while continuing to whisk. Keep that up until you notice a change in texture of the mixture--it starts to get a little stiff. Usually you see this when about a third of the oil is in there. At that point, you can add the oil in a thin stream, continuing to whisk. If at any point it looks as if the oil isn't being incorporated, stop adding oil until your whisking gets it in there. Keep going until all the oil is used.
Makes about one cup.

Come Forth Erato

My best hours in my kitchen
Are those when my muse joins me
My mind overflows with ingredients and poetic thoughts
Each component in the recipe is carefully selected
The seasonings tend to blend and become empowered
The lettuces are always crisp and fresh
The dressing is light with just the right tang
I welcome these occasions
And pray for Erato when I enter the kitchen

Brunch, Eggs And Cheese

BRS Huevos Rancheros

2 corn tortillas
1 avocado
1 teaspoon lime juice (fresh)
1 cup salsa
1 cup refried black beans
2 eggs
2 dollops sour cream
2 tablespoons shredded cheddar or Monterey Jack cheese

For homemade salsa:
1 tomato, chopped
½ onion, chopped
1 clove garlic, minced
½ jalapeño pepper, chopped

Heat tortillas directly on stovetop for one or two minutes and set aside on warmed plate. Mash avocado with lime juice and set aside. Place one tortilla on each plate, coat tortillas completely with refried beans. Meanwhile, fry your eggs in the skillet, season to taste, then place eggs on top of refried bean topped tortilla. Pour warmed salsa over the eggs, then top with more shredded Cheddar or Monterey Jack cheese, a dollop of sour cream and a dollop of avocado mashed with 1 teaspoon of lime juice.

Prepare salsa, by sautéing onion, garlic, and tomato. Toss cilantro in at end of cooking. Keep warm. Bottled salsa can be substituted for the homemade.

Creamy Scrambled Eggs

8 eggs
¼ cup whole milk
¼ teaspoon salt
¼ teaspoon freshly ground black pepper
1 tablespoon butter
4 ounces cream cheese, cut into small cubes
3 tablespoons chopped fresh chives, divided
sprigs of chives and chive blossoms, for garnish

In a large bowl beat the eggs, milk, salt, freshly ground black pepper, and 1 tablespoon chives. Melt butter in a large non-stick pan and, when hot, add egg mixture. Cook like standard scrambled eggs, but when about ½ set, add cubes of cream cheese. When the eggs are finished cooking, the cheese will be melted. Divide eggs on serving plate(s). Sprinkle remaining chopped chives around the perimeter of the plate and use cropped sprigs of chives and blossoms as additional garnish.

French Apple Toast

12 slices of bread - white or whole-wheat
4 or 5 granny smith apples, peeled and sliced thin
½ cup water
1 teaspoon cinnamon
1 tablespoon sugar
¾ cup brown sugar
3 tablespoons light corn syrup
3 tablespoons butter
1 cup pecans
3 eggs
1 ¼ cups milk
1 teaspoon vanilla
¼ teaspoon nutmeg

Slice apples and boil 5 minutes in ½ cup water and drain.
Combine with 1 tsp cinnamon and 1 tbsp sugar. Set aside. Cook brown sugar, corn syrup, and butter in skillet until mixture begins to boil. Pour into 13 x 9 pan. Spread on a lot of whole pecans - a cup or more. Place 6 slices of bread in pan. Arrange apple slices on top of bread. Put 6 slices of bread on top of the apples. Whisk together eggs, milk, vanilla, and nutmeg. Pour over bread. Refrigerate overnight. Bake uncovered for 35-45 min at 325°.

Contributor: Linda Krueger, Maple Inn, Chautauqua, NY

Betty Ruth's Brunch Torte

Pimiento Layer:
1 (8 oz) can pimientos

Spinach Layer:
2 pounds spinach, fresh
1 clove garlic
3 shallots
2 egg whites
3 tablespoons unsalted butter
¾ teaspoon salt
freshly ground pepper
nutmeg, grated
1 dash hot sauce

Egg And Cheese Layer:
1 dozen eggs
¼ pound Swiss cheese, grated
¼ pound Parmesan cheese, grated
3 shallots
3 slices firm white bread
3 scallions
½ cup parsley
½ cup milk
freshly ground pepper
½ teaspoon salt
1 pinch tarragon
1 dash hot sauce
4 tablespoons unsalted butter

Ham Layer:
2 large egg whites
1 tablespoons Dijon
¾ pound lean ham

Pimiento Mixture: Preheat oven to 250 °. Drain the pimientos, slice them into wide strips, then bake for 20 minutes on cookie sheet to dry. Set aside.

Spinach Mixture: Cook spinach over high heat in boiling water just to cover and wilt. As spinach wilts, plunge into cold water to stop the cooking process, drain and wring out in towels, until completely dry. There should be 2 cups dry spinach. With machine running, drop shallots and garlic through tube. Process spinach, egg whites, butter and seasonings to a puree. Transfer to a bowl and reserve.

Ham Mixture: Process egg whites, mustard and ham cubes, turning machine on and off until ham is coarsely chopped. Mixture should resemble coarsely chopped hamburger. Set aside.

Egg And Cheese Mixture: Cover raw unbroken eggs with very warm water (140 °) and let stand 10 to 15 minutes. Shred Swiss cheese, using light pressure. Set aside. Grate Parmesan, add to Swiss. Set aside. Process bread, parsley and scallions until finely minced. Transfer to a mixing bowl and add milk and let soak just until liquid is absorbed. Push this mixture to side of bowl with a spoon and draining off excess liquid. Add eggs and seasonings to processor bowl and process for 10 seconds. Melt butter in a 10 inch or larger skillet, over medium-low heat. Add mixture all at once. Stir continually with flat side of fork just until they are no longer runny. Remove from heat. Add soaked crumbs, 3/4 of cheese mixture.

Assembly: Adjust oven rack to center. Preheat oven to 400°. Butter springform pan. Place half of the egg mixture in the pan. Spread firmly and evenly with a spatula. Cover with half of the spinach mixture, then with the ham. Smooth each layer firmly with spatula. Place pimiento slices evenly over the ham, making sure some slices are placed around the outer edge to enhance the appearance. Top the pimiento layer with the remaining spinach and then remaining eggs. Sprinkle evenly with reserved cheeses. (Can be prepared ahead to this point and refrigerated, even the night before). Bake for 30 minutes. Let rest for 20 minutes. Carefully run knife around edges. Remove springform and transfer torte on pan bottom to serving dish.

*To accompany this torte, I select a fresh pineapple with nice fronds, cut off and reserve top (about 1 inch down from leaf base) and scoop out a well in remaining base. I place the pineapple on a large platter, fill the well with poppy seed dressing and surround the pineapple with skewered fresh fruit (6 inch bamboo skewers) and place the pineapple top on edge of try to enhance the presentation.

Peeper's Peepers
Corned Beef with Nested Eggs

3 cans corned beef hash
Worcestershire
6 eggs
freshly ground pepper
salt

Spread corned beef evenly in a buttered quiche dish. Sprinkle with Worcestershire. Make 6 wells with back of spoon. Bake in a 375° oven until top browns. Put eggs in wells, sprinkle eggs with salt and freshly ground black pepper, return to oven until eggs set. Garnish with parsley. Serve with toast and chutney.

If you are only serving two, you can prepare this as above using 1 can of corned beef and two eggs. Divide the corned beef and place it in two 3 ½ to 4 inch ramekins and proceed as above.

This makes a quick and easy breakfast surprise. I usually serve it with toast and a Melon Boat (*see recipe page 260).

*This is a favorite of my wonderful friend and colleague, Dr. Quinn Peeper

Eggs in a Ham Nest

2 (4 ½ oz) cans deviled ham
1/4 teaspoon Tabasco, divided
2 tablespoons Parmesan
1 tablespoons parsley
½ teaspoon salt
6 slices bread, toasted
6 eggs, separated

Mix ham, ⅛ teaspoon, Tabasco and parsley. Spread on toasted bread. Separate eggs, putting yolks back in shells in egg cartons. Beat whites until stiff, but not dry. Fold in cheese. Spoon whites onto ham spread, make nest and slide in yolk. Add remaining Tabasco. Bake for 10 minutes at 350° or until yolks set.

Frittata Alla Veneta

1 clove garlic
olive oil
1 bunch parsley, ground
6 anchovies, cut into pieces
¾ pound tomatoes, peeled and seeded
salt
freshly ground pepper
10 eggs

Crush a clove of garlic and brown it in a tablespoon of oil in a pot. While it's coloring, grind a small bunch of parsley in a mortar with six boned anchovies, cut into pieces. Stir this mixture into the pot, together with ¾ pound blenched peeled seeded tomatoes. Season with salt and pepper to taste and cook the mixture for 8-10 minutes over a moderate flame, then set it aside and let it cool. In the mean time lightly beat ten eggs in a bowl. Stir the cool tomato mixture into the eggs, heat a tablespoon of oil in a skillet until it almost smokes, and pour in the eggs. Stir the mixture around for a few seconds and cook it until the bottom is set and it begins to firm up. Flip it onto a lid or plate, wipe the skillet clean with a paper towel, heat another tablespoon of oil in it, and slide the frittata back into the skillet to brown the other side Cook a few minutes more and it's done! Serves 4-6

Frittata with Cheese, Sun-Dried Tomatoes, and Basil

10 large eggs
¼ cup whipping cream
1 ½ cups crumbled feta cheese
10 oil-packed sun-dried tomatoes, drained and finely chopped
4 green onions, thinly sliced
⅓ cup fresh basil leaves, finely chopped
½ teaspoon salt
¼ teaspoon freshly ground pepper
¼ cup (½ stick) butter
⅓ cup pitted Kalamata olives, thinly sliced
3 tablespoons freshly grated Parmesan cheese

Preheat broiler. Whisk eggs and cream in large bowl to blend. Stir in feta cheese, tomatoes, onions, basil, salt, and freshly ground black pepper. Melt butter in large ovenproof nonstick skillet over medium-high heat. Add egg mixture; do not stir. Cook until eggs start to get firm and sides and bottom begin to brown, lifting sides occasionally to let uncooked egg run underneath, about 5 minutes. Sprinkle with olives and Parmesan cheese. Transfer skillet to broiler and cook until eggs start to puff and brown, about 2 minutes. Slide out onto plate. Slice frittata into wedges. Serve warm or at room temperature.
Yield: 4 to 6 servings

Sausage and Cheese Strata with Sun-Dried Tomatoes

½ cup sun-dried tomatoes (not oil packed), chopped
12 ounces hot Italian sausage, casing removed, crumbled
3 ½ cups milk (do not use low-fat or nonfat)
8 large eggs
2 teaspoons minced fresh thyme or ¾ teaspoon dried
1 ½ teaspoons salt
¼ teaspoon freshly ground pepper
11 slices white sandwich bread crusts trimmed, cut into 1-inch pieces
½ cup chopped onion
½ cup freshly grated parmesan cheese
1 cup (packed) grated mozzarella cheese
¼ cup crumbled soft fresh goat cheese (such as Montrachet)
fresh parsley, chopped

Place sun-dried tomatoes in medium bowl. Pour enough boiling water over to cover. Let stand until softened, about 15 minutes. Drain. Sauté sausages in heavy medium skillet over medium heat until cooked through, breaking up with back of spoon, about 5 minutes. Using slotted spoon, transfer sausage to paper towels and drain well. Butter 13x9x2-inch glass baking dish. Whisk milk, eggs, thyme, salt, and freshly ground black pepper in large bowl to blend. Add sun-dried tomatoes, sausage, bread, onion, and Parmesan cheese, then stir to blend. Transfer to prepared dish. Cover and refrigerate at least 4 hours or overnight. Preheat oven to 375°. Bake strata uncovered until puffed and golden brown, about 45 minutes. Sprinkle with mozzarella and goat cheese and bake until mozzarella melts, about 5 minutes. Transfer pan to rack and cool 5 minutes. Sprinkle with parsley. Yield: serves 8.

Pain Perdu

1 large egg
⅛ teaspoon cinnamon
½ cup milk
6 slices old bread
2 teaspoon syrup, honey or sugar
1 teaspoon vanilla
1 tablespoon oil for skillet or grill

Mix all ingredients (except oil). Dip bread in mixture. Grill in skillet or on stovetop griddle.

Cracked Eggshell

My eggshell is cracked
A monster tread upon me
First the albumen flowed out in tears
Now the yolk lies trapped inside the shattered shell.

How can I get it out?
As long as it remains inside
It blocks the way for cleansing and restoration
I know that I can never again be a whole egg.

However, if I can deliver the yolk
Maybe I can dry out inside
Once dry I shall work with the shattered shell
And try to make a new panoramic egg of it.

Maybe it will be ready by Easter
Hopefully, when one peeps inside they will see
Only beautiful memories and tranquility
No questions, no regrets, no guilt nor anger.

Seafood

Creamed Seafood in Puff Pastry Fish

1 (12 oz) package frozen puff pastry
2 tablespoons butter
2 green onions
½ teaspoon fresh dill
2 tablespoons flour
¾ cup warm milk
1 tablespoon lemon juice
salt
¾ pound small bay shrimp, cooked and peeled
1 egg, beaten with a little water
¼ cup heavy cream

To make puff pastry fish: Preheat oven to 375°. Let the two sheets of frozen puff pastry thaw a few minutes until pliable. Unfold, brush top of 1 piece lightly with water. Lay other piece on top (do not try to press together). Cut out fish shapes with a vol-au-vent cutter (Wms-Sonoma product). You should get four or five fish per the doubled sheets. Place on a baking sheet, brush tops with beaten egg and bake 20 to 25 minutes until golden brown. Remove from oven, place on a cooling rack. Remove top part of center section carefully using tip of a sharp knife to loosen margins and put aside for lid. Scoop out the inside of the pastry shells. Set pastry aside until serving time. These can be made ahead (even a few days) and kept in a tin until needed. Can be refreshed by placing in a hot oven for a few minutes and re-cooling.

To make seafood filling: Melt butter in a sauce pan. Sauté the onion and dill, stir in the flour and let cook for a few seconds. Whisking vigorously, add the warmed milk slowly, and let cook for 1 or 2 minutes over low heat until thickened. Stir in the lemon juice and season with salt and freshly ground black pepper. Add the shrimp or crab and cook for 1 or 2 minutes, add cream and cook another minute. Check seasoning. Place a puff pastry fish on each plate. Spoon in the seafood mixture, put on tops and sprinkle with parsley. Good with salad of tomatoes, fresh basil and Montrachet. Yield: 4 servings

Issy King's Shrimp

2 pounds shrimp with heads on
3 tablespoons salt
1 heavy iron pot with lid

Heat iron pot until very hot over medium heat. While heating pot, wash shrimp in colander and immediately put them in hot pot and put lid on. Cook for exactly 2 minutes, lift cover and stir. If all are pink they are done. If not, cook 1 or 2 minutes more. Drain in colander, reserve liquid for gumbo or other use. Sprinkle drained shrimp with 2 to 3 tablespoons of salt (or Old Bay Seasoning), stirring around well.
Salt rule: 1 tablespoon per pound and 1 for the pot!
*Old Bay Seasoning can be used instead of salt

Shrimp Bonne Femme or L'Ancienne

6 dozen shrimp, peeled and deveined
cracker meal
4 ounces butter
1 lemon
6 green onions, chopped
½ pound fresh mushrooms, very finely sliced
2 tablespoons very finely chopped parsley
1 cup dry white wine
1 cup Béchamel Sauce (*see recipe page 269)

Lightly bread the shrimp in cracker meal. Sauté in 4 oz melted butter. Add the juice of 1 lemon. Prepare the sauce: sauté in butter the onions, mushrooms, and parsley. Add 1 cup of dry white wine and 1 cup of béchamel sauce to mixture and pour over shrimp.

Source: Filippo from The Pillars

Paella

4 pounds frying chicken pieces (remove skin before cooking)
¼ cup olive oil
salt
freshly ground pepper
flour
¼ cup water
1 tsp oregano
2 cups chopped onion
2 cloves garlic, minced
1 pound chorizo sausage, sliced
2 cups long grain rice (or 2 packages paella mix)
4 cups chicken broth
¼ teaspoon saffron
1 can artichoke hearts, quartered
2 cups green peas
1 (28 oz) can tomatoes, drain and chop
1 (7 oz) can pimientos, cut into strips
1 pound shrimp, shelled
24 clams, steamed beforehand
3 (1 pound) live lobsters, steamed beforehand

Heat olive oil in large iron skillet (with cover for later use). Salt and pepper chicken and dust lightly with flour. Brown well in olive oil. Add ¼ cup water and 1 teaspoon oregano to chicken, cover and cook over low heat for 30 minutes. Remove chicken pieces. Add onion and garlic to skillet and sauté for 5 minutes, stirring frequently. Set sautéed onion and garlic aside. Brown sausage in same skillet. Remove sausage and add to onion mixture. Add rice to skillet and cook until transparent. Add chicken broth and saffron, cover and cook for 15 minutes. Check for seasonings (salt and pepper). Rub inside of paella pan with olive oil, add artichokes and peas. Mix onion and sausage with rice, gently toss rice with the vegetables in paella dish, adding tomatoes and pimiento. Top with the chicken pieces. Mix shrimp into paella mix. Bake for 30 minutes at 325°. Top with lobster claws, chunks of lobster and clams. Serve with green salad or avocado boat, white wine, and flan.

Shrimp de Jonghe

2 pounds shrimp, shelled
2 cloves garlic, minced
dash freshly grated nutmeg
hint of powdered mace
1 tablespoons fresh chopped parsley
hint of grated lemon rind
1 tablespoon chopped shallots
1 tablespoon chopped chives
salt
freshly ground pepper
½ teaspoon dried French tarragon
pinch of dried thyme
1 stick unsalted butter at room temperature
1 bay leaf
1 ½ cups bread crumbs
½ cup sherry

Preheat oven to 400°. Mix together the garlic, herbs, and spices and work well into the butter. Add the breadcrumbs and sherry, then salt and pepper to taste. Let this mixture sit at least an hour to "hatch". Cook shrimp in boiling water with a bay leaf for 3 minutes, drain. Butter an ovenproof dish, put half the flavored mixture on the bottom, and then press shrimp gently into it. Top with other half of mix. Bake for 10 minutes, then put under broiler until the top browns. You can easily prepare this in advance and refrigerate it, but be sure that it is back to room temperature before you put it in the oven.

Shrimp Stuffed Eggplant

1 large eggplant
olive oil
1 onion, sliced
1 shallot
2 stalks celery
2 cloves garlic
½ bell pepper
1 egg
6 stuffed olives, chopped
1 cup breadcrumbs
1 teaspoon salt
¼ teaspoon cayenne
¼ teaspoon Old Bay Seasoning
½ teaspoon freshly ground pepper
¼ teaspoon thyme
½ teaspoon rosemary
1 teaspoon chopped parsley
1 pounds shrimp, peeled
¼ cup fresh Parmesan
½ cup coarse breadcrumbs for topping

Preheat oven to 350°. Cut eggplant in half lengthwise. Brush pulp with olive oil and place pulp-side down on baking tray. Bake for thirty minutes. When cool enough to handle, remove pulp with spoon, being careful to keep shell intact. Sauté onion, shallot, celery, garlic, and bell pepper until softened. Combine eggplant pulp with vegetable mixture, a beaten egg, chopped olives, breadcrumbs, and seasonings. Add peeled, raw shrimp. Mix coarse breadcrumbs and parmesan and sprinkle over top. Bake for 30 to 40 minutes.
Yield: 2 servings

Aegean Shrimp

¼ cup olive oil
1 onion, chopped
¾ lb tomatoes, chopped (2 medium tomatoes)
2 cloves garlic, crushed
1 small bay leaf
¼ teaspoon dried basil
1 teaspoon dried oregano
½ cup chopped fresh parsley
¼ teaspoon hot sesame oil (do not substitute)
salt
freshly ground black pepper
1 pound raw shrimp
8 ounce feta cheese
8 Kalamata olives,
½ lemon, squeezed

Preheat oven to 475º. Sauté onion in oil over medium heat until soft. Add tomatoes, garlic, bay leaf, basil, oregano, parsley, hot sesame oil, salt and freshly ground black pepper. Cook 4 minutes. Remove vegetables from skillet with slotted spoon and place in bottom 8 x 8 x 2 baking dish. Bring skillet juices to a boil and add peeled shrimp. Cook 2 minutes or until shrimp are pink. Add shrimp to vegetables; crumble feta over top. Arrange olives on top and squeeze lemon juice over all. Bake 10-15 minutes. Serve over rice or grits. Serves: 4

Artichoke-Crabmeat Casserole

1 large can artichoke hearts
1 pound crabmeat
½ pound fresh mushrooms
4 tablespoons butter
1 cup cream
½ teaspoon salt
1 teaspoon Worcestershire
¼ cup med dry sherry
dash paprika
dash cayenne
pepper to taste
½ cup Parmesan, grated

Put artichokes in bottom of casserole and top with crabmeat. Sauté the mushrooms in the butter and remove with slotted spoon and add to casserole. Add cream, salt, Worcestershire, sherry, paprika, cayenne, and pepper (to taste) to butter in skillet to make cream sauce. Pour over crabmeat. Top with Parmesan and bake for 20 minutes at 375°.

Betty Ruth's Crab Ramekins

1 pound crabmeat, lump or back fin
1 egg white, lightly beaten
1 tablespoon all-purpose flour
1 tablespoon butter
½ cup milk
2 green onions, minced
1 teaspoon freshly ground black pepper
¼ teaspoon cayenne
1 teaspoon sea salt
1 tablespoon sherry
½ cup grated gruyere cheese (optional)
lemon wedges

Carefully pick crabmeat, removing all shell. Pour the egg white over the crabmeat and set aside. Melt the butter, stir in the flour and cook for 1-2 minutes. Then whisk in the milk to make a cream sauce. Add the minced onions, black pepper, cayenne, 1 tsp salt and sherry to the sauce. Gently fold the crabmeat into the mixture and divide among 6 ramekins or shells. If desired, each can be topped with grated cheese before baking. Serve with lemon wedges. Bake for 10 minutes at 375°.

Serves 6

Crabmeat au Gratin

3 tablespoons butter
3 tablespoons flour
2 cups milk
½ cup dry sherry
1 teaspoon Worcestershire sauce
1 teaspoon seasoned salt, or to taste
1 pound lump crabmeat
½ cup shredded cheddar cheese
½ cup shredded Monterey Jack cheese
paprika

Preheat oven to 350°. Melt butter in a saucepan. Add flour and stir to mix thoroughly. Add milk, sherry, Worcestershire sauce, and seasoned salt, stirring constantly. Bring to a boil, continue stirring and cook for 5 minutes. Remove from heat. Sauce may be refrigerated at this point, if desired. Mix sauce with crabmeat and divide among individual ramekins or spoon into a buttered ceramic baking dish. Top with a mixture of the two cheeses and sprinkle with paprika. Bake about 15 minutes for ramekins or 30 minutes for 1 large dish. Allow additional cooking time if the sauce has been refrigerated.
Yield: 4 to 6 servings

Soft-shell Crab Menuniere

12 soft-shell crabs
¼ cup butter
3 eggs, beaten
1 lemon
½ cup milk
¼ cup beef stock
flour seasoned with salt and pepper

Wash crabs well and pat dry. Beat eggs with milk. Dip crabs in seasoned flour, then in beaten eggs. Heat butter in a large skillet and sauté crabs quickly until golden brown on both sides. Squeeze lemon over crabs. Transfer to a serving plate. Add beef stock to butter and lemon juice left In pan. Bring to a boil over high heat, scraping up any browned bits in the pan. Pour over crabs and serve with lemon wedges.

Amsac Oysters

2 dozen oysters
1 cup chopped scallions
½ cup chopped mushrooms
2 tablespoons butter
salt
freshly ground black pepper
red black pepper
2 tablespoons flour
½ cup dry white wine
oyster liquor
milk
fresh dry bread crumbs
grated Kasseri cheese

Drain oysters, saving liquor for sauce. Sauté scallions and mushrooms in butter. Add all seasonings, then flour. Blend well and cook for 1 minute. Stir in wine and oyster liquor to make thick sauce, thinning as necessary with milk. Top each oyster on the half shell with some sauce. Mix Kasseri and bread crumbs and sprinkle on top. Bake 10 minutes at 400°, then quickly brown under broiler.

Elmira's Oyster Dressing

1 skillet cornbread, made a day or so ahead
1 pan biscuits, made a day or so ahead
1 bunch celery, chopped
3 onions, chopped
juice from turkey
lemon pepper
sage
1 quart oysters, with liquor saved
salt to taste
freshly ground black pepper to taste

Tear cornbread and biscuits into pieces and toast. Cook onion and celery in enough water to cover. This softens the onion and celery. Mix breads with vegetables and seasonings to taste. Add oysters and enough of juice from oysters to make a soupy mix. Cook in a 2-inch-deep dressing pan at 350° until crispy, but not dried out. For allergic or "no-oyster" friends, you can bake a small side pan of plain dressing without oysters.
Contributor: Elmira

Grilled Shucked Oysters

2 dozen shucked oysters
¼ cup salt
freshly ground black pepper
flour in a shaker
melted butter
lemon wedges

Preheat the grill for 15 minutes. Place the oysters in a platter and sprinkle lightly with salt and freshly ground black pepper. Dust lightly and evenly with flour. Turn over carefully and repeat on the other side. Place the oysters in hinged grill and fasten the grill securely. Drizzle one side with melted butter and place on the heated grill buttered side down. Grill for 5 minutes. Drizzle the upper side with butter and turn over. Grill for 5 minutes second side. Serve with lemon wedges.

Pan-Roasted Oysters

2 ounces pancetta, finely diced or 2 oz Tasso
1 tablespoon butter
½ cup onion, finely chopped
½ cup celery, finely chopped
 salt and pepper
½ cup dry vermouth
2 cups half and half
1 teaspoon Worcestershire sauce
3 dozen oysters, shucked

Fry pancetta or Tasso in a deep saucepan until translucent, but not crisp. Add onions and celery and sprinkle with salt and pepper. Add the vermouth and cook until reduced and thickened. Add the half and half and Worcestershire sauce. Bring to a simmer and cook until reduced by one-third. Strain the oysters and add their liquor to the pan. Cook a few minutes. Add oysters and cook until the edges just start to curl. Serve with slices of crusty bread or crisp toast points (crusts removed).

Oyster Rockefeller Casserole

1 quart raw oysters
1 stick butter
1 rib celery, finely chopped
1 medium onion, chopped
½ cup parsley, finely chopped
1 pound fresh spinach, chopped or frozen spinach, thawed and finely chopped and drained
¼ teaspoon anise seed
¼ cup Worcestershire
½ cup soft bread crumbs
salt
freshly ground black pepper
cayenne
toasted bread or cracker crumbs
½ cup grated Parmesan cheese

Preheat oven to 450°. Butter a casserole dish. Drain oysters and arrange in one layer in casserole. Melt butter and sauté celery and onions until they begin to soften. Combine with parsley, spinach, anise seed, Worcestershire, soft bread crumbs, salt, and cayenne. Spread this mixture over the oysters. Bake for 30 minutes. Remove; if necessary, pour off water that has cooked from oysters. Sprinkle with grated cheese and a thin layer of the bread or cracker crumbs. Return to oven for 10 minutes until slightly brown.
Yield: 6 servings

Sophia Clikas' Oyster Pie

1 tube crackers
1 green onion, minced
1 stick butter
1 pint oysters, drain
dash Tabasco

Crumble crackers with hand; add to melted butter. Add other ingredients, except oysters, and toss with fork. Line bottom of pie pan with ⅔ of crumb mixture, cover with oysters. Top with other ⅓ of crumb mixture. Bake 350° for 30 minutes.
Yield: 2 servings

Chafing Dish Oysters

1 quart oysters, undrained
¼ cup butter
1 8 ounce package cream cheese, softened
6 tablespoons dry white wine
3 tablespoons scallions, chopped
½ teaspoon paprika
½ teaspoon anchovy paste
¼ teaspoon cayenne
¼ teaspoon salt
6 drops Tabasco
parsley, chopped
4 dozen patty shells or Croustades (*see recipe page 10)

Place undrained oysters in saucepan. Cook over medium heat for 2 minutes or until edges curl. Combine butter and cream cheese in a medium saucepan. Place over low heat. When melted, add wine and whisk. Stir in scallions, paprika, anchovy paste, cayenne, salt, and Tabasco. Bring to a boil over high heat, stirring constantly. Gently fold in coarsely chopped oysters. Put in a chafing dish. Garnish with parsley.

Grilled Oysters

1 dozen oysters on half shell
1 cup grated Parmesan cheese
1 cup grated Romano cheese
1 tablespoon dried parsley
1 stick butter, melted
2 teaspoons fresh garlic, minced
salt
freshly ground black pepper

Combine cheeses and parsley and set aside. Place oysters over hot fire and top each oyster with 1 tablespoon of garlic butter sauce (melted butter, minced garlic and salt to taste) and cook for 2 minutes. Top with 1 tablespoon cheese mixture and cook 5-7 minutes more until cheese melts a bit.

Coquilles St. Jacques

2 pounds scallops
1 cup dry white wine
¼ cup shallots, chopped
1 clove garlic, crushed
1 bay leaf
½ teaspoon salt
¼ teaspoon freshly ground pepper
9 tablespoons butter
2 cups fresh mushrooms, sliced
3 tablespoons flour
¾ cup milk
2 tablespoons lemon juice
¼ teaspoon dried thyme
2 egg yolks
¼ cup heavy cream
¾ cup shredded Swiss cheese
1 cup fresh bread crumbs

Quickly rinse scallops under cold running water and drain. Cut, if large. Combine wine, shallots, garlic, bay leaf, salt, and freshly ground black pepper. Bring to a boil. Add scallops, return just to a boil, then reduce heat. Simmer 5 minutes until scallops are tender and opaque. Remove scallops with a slotted spoon. Increase heat to high. Boil liquid until reduced to 1 cup, strain and set aside. In medium skillet, melt 2 tablespoons butter. Remove from heat, add bread crumbs, and toss. Set aside in a small bowl. In same skillet, sauté mushrooms in 4 tablespoons of butter for 5 minutes or until tender. Remove with slotted spoon and add to scallops.

Make wine sauce: Melt remaining butter in skillet, blend in flour and cook for 1 minute. Remove from heat, stir in 1 cup reserved liquid, ¾ cup milk, lemon juice, salt, and thyme. Cook, stirring constantly until sauce thickens and comes to a boil, Boil 2 minutes. Beat 2 egg yolks with the heavy cream stir ½ cup of the hot sauce into the egg mixture, and then stir all into remaining sauce in the skillet. Cook, stirring constantly for 2 minutes. Remove from heat, pour over scallops and mushrooms. Mix gently until well combined. Divide mixture into 6 scallop shells. Sprinkle tops with grated cheese and bread crumbs. Broil 6 inches from flame for 3 to 4 minutes or until bubbling at edges and crumbs slightly browned. If these are cold, may need a quick heating in the oven before going under the broiler.

Yield: 6 servings

Prosciutto-Wrapped Scallops with Rosemary

1 ½ pounds scallops
30 fresh rosemary sprigs (each 3 to 4 inches long)
3 ounces prosciutto, sliced paper thin
3 to 4 tablespoons extra-virgin olive oil
1 lemon, cut in half
sea salt
freshly ground black pepper

Strip the bottom leaves off the rosemary sprigs. Cut the prosciutto into strips just large enough to wrap around the scallops (about ¾ by 3½ inches). Lay a scallop flat on your work surface. Wrap a piece of prosciutto around it and skewer it with a rosemary sprig. Prepare the remaining scallops the same way. Arrange the scallops on a plate or in a baking dish. Drizzle them on both sides with olive oil; squeeze a little lemon juice over them. Season lightly with salt and pepper (use the salt sparingly, as the prosciutto is fairly salty). Let marinate for 15 minutes, while you light the grill. Set up the grill for direct grilling and preheat to high. If you have a fish or vegetable grate, place it on top and preheat as well. Brush and oil the grate. Grill the scallops until just cooked through, 2 to 3 minutes per side. Serve at once.

Frog Legs Persillade

8 pair small frog legs
1 ½ cup buttermilk
1 teaspoon green Tabasco
1 cup flour
1 tablespoon salt
¼ teaspoon white pepper
¼ teaspoon thyme
2 sticks butter
1 teaspoon red wine vinegar
Garnish: lemon halves

Persille sauce:
2 tablespoons extra-virgin olive oil
6 cloves garlic, chopped
15 sprigs flat-leaf parsley, leaves only, chopped
¼ teaspoon salt
1 clove garlic, crushed

1. Wash the frog's legs, marinate them in the refrigerator for two hours in a food storage bag with the buttermilk and the tabasco.
2. For the persille sauce, heat the olive oil in a small saucepan over medium-low heat. Add the chopped garlic and parsley. Cook until the parsley is wilted and the garlic is fragrant. Remove from the heat. Scoop the pan contents into a small food processor, blender, or (most effective) mortar and pestle. Add ¼ teaspoon salt and puree the mixture. Spoon the mixture into one corner of a small plastic bag (like a sandwich bag).
3. Combine the flour, salt, white pepper and thyme in a wide bowl. Shake the excess buttermilk off the frog's legs. Coat them lightly with the flour mixture.

4. Heat the butter in a medium skillet over medium-high heat. When it's melted, add the crushed garlic clove. When the butter is bubbling, add the frog's legs and sauté until golden, turning once. Remove and drain the frog's legs. Whisk in the vinegar.

5. Place the frog's legs on serving plates. Spoon the butter from the pan onto the plates, trying to avoid picking up the solids on the bottom of the pan.

6. With scissors, snip off the corner of the plastic bag with the parsley mixture. Squeeze out lines of the persille across the frog legs. Garnish with lemon halves.

**Frog legs are delicious. The smaller they are the better. As a child I went "frog gigging" with my father and was taught how to clean frog legs by "pulling their pants down". Mine come from the market today, fully "undressed"!

Frog Legs Belle Meuniere

8 pair medium frog legs
salt
freshly ground pepper
¼ cup shallots, chopped
¼ cup sliced mushrooms
¼ cup white wine
1 lemon, juiced
3 teaspoons cognac
1 tablespoon chopped parsley

Separate frog legs and season with salt and pepper. Sauté slowly in butter until brown. Add shallots and mushrooms and simmer 10 minutes. Add wine and lemon, simmer 5 minutes. Stir in cognac and sprinkle with chopped parsley.
Yield: 4

Crayfish Etouffee

3 pounds crayfish - tails and yellow fat
1 stick butter
4 tablespoons flour
2 bay leaves
Tony's Creole Seasoning
1 tablespoon Worcestershire
¼ teaspoon Tabasco
¼ teaspoon cayenne
2 tablespoons paprika
1 large onion, chopped
1 bell pepper, chopped
4 stalks celery, chopped
2 cloves garlic, minced
1 cup water
1 bottle clam juice
¼ cup tomato paste
2 tablespoons lemon juice
2 green onion stems, minced for garnish
2 tablespoons chopped parsley
1 ½ tablespoons cornstarch (optional)
hot cooked rice

Melt butter and crayfish fat, add flour to make roux. Cook slowly until chestnut brown. Add seasonings. Add vegetables and cook until tender, then add clam juice and water. Add crayfish tails and simmer for 30 to 40 minutes. Just before serving, stir in lemon juice. Serve over cooked rice. Garnish with onion tops and parsley.

If a lighter, red etouffee is preferred, omit flour and sauté vegetables in butter. Season tails with Tony's Creole and quickly sauté. Proceed with recipe. If thickening is desired, towards end of cooking mix in 1 ½ tablespoons cornstarch dissolved in a small amount of water.

Yield: 4 servings

Arthur Britton's King Mackerel

2 king mackerel, filets, leaving skin on
6 lemons, juiced
¼ bottle Worcestershire
2 onions, chopped
1 stick butter
sprinkle sugar
sprinkle salt

Mix all ingredients for sauce and simmer. Put fish on foil and place on grill, skin side down. Cook about 20 minutes, basting frequently, with lid down. Serve with slaw or salad, boiled corn and hush puppies.

Note: When I was teaching residents, Wednesday was "fishing" day for a lucky resident chosen by Dr. O.M. Otts, Jr. After work, we they would gather at my home to enjoy the catch of the day. This is Arthur Britton's catch and recipe.

Source: Arthur Britton May 1977

Grilled Salmon with Honey Mustard Glaze

6 ounce salmon fillet, brushed with oil
2 tablespoons honey
2 pinches dry Coleman's mustard
2 tablespoons warm water
2 teaspoons soy sauce
salt to taste
1 pinch freshly ground pepper

Prepare Honey-Mustard Glaze: In a bowl, combine honey, mustard, water, and soy sauce. Salt and freshly ground black pepper to taste. Brush one six-ounce salmon fillet lightly with oil, season with salt and freshly ground black pepper. Grill each side for 2-3 minutes. Turn the fish over carefully only once to mark the surface; cook to desired texture. Brush flesh side of fish with glaze before removing from grill. Serve at once.

Note: Dr. Dan and Rita Thompson taught me to prepare salmon as we sailed and grilled aboard Brer' Rabbit on Lake Lanier.

Salmon with Maple Rum Glaze

2 (6 ounces) salmon filets
¼ ounce rum
1 ounce corn syrup (Karo)
1 tablespoon brown sugar
2 tablespoons of cream

Mix rum, corn syrup, brown sugar and cream. Lightly salt and pepper salmon filets. Brush glaze on salmon. Grill for 2-3 minutes. Brush glaze on flesh side of salmon, turn and grill for 2-3 minutes. Contributor: Gray Fobes, The Colony

Tilapia on a Bed of Spinach

1 tilapia filet
1 cup chopped spinach, fresh or frozen
1 teaspoon lemon zest
2 teaspoons lemon juice
½ teaspoon lemon pepper
3 sun-dried tomatoes, in oil
3 slices fresh mozzarella cheese
1 ½ tablespoons grated Parmesan cheese
salt to taste
freshly ground black pepper to taste
½ cup dry white wine

Preheat oven to 425°. Make bed of spinach in au gratin dish. Sprinkle with lemon zest, lemon pepper, and lemon juice. Rinse sun-dried tomatoes, pat dry, then coarsely dice and sprinkle over the bed of spinach. Top with mozzarella slices. Place tilapia on top and season with salt and freshly ground black pepper. Sprinkle parmesan on top of fish. Pour wine over all and bake for 20 minutes. Contributor: Michael Harold

BRS Flounder with Capers and Scallions

1 whole flounder (with head on and skin intact)
freshly ground black pepper
salt
olive oil
1 lemon
fresh parsley, minced
2 scallions, minced
1 tablespoon capers

Sprinkle flounder all over with salt and freshly ground black pepper, rub with oil. Score flounder and squeeze lemon juice liberally over fish. Stuff scored slits with mixture of fresh parsley, capers and scallions. Bake in a 350 °F oven for 30 minutes, then run under broiler to crisp. To score flounder, make diagonal cuts approximately ½ inch deep (crisscross the cuts).

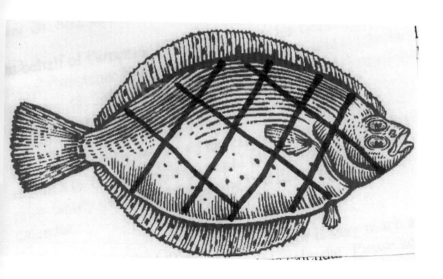

Cook On

Cook on old withered one

As a child you were taught that:

There is a Santa Claus

If you are good and obey the ten commandments they will take you

through this life to life eternal

The way to a man's heart is through his stomach

Now you have experienced life almost seven decades.

What have you learned?

There is no Santa Claus

This is eternity

The way to a man's heart is not through his stomach.

Poultry & Game

Chicken Curry

1 (4 pound) chicken
2 cups onions, chopped
5 granny smith apples, chopped
2 tablespoons curry
⅔ cup chicken fat or butter
2 ½ cups chicken stock, hot
2 teaspoons guava jelly
salt to taste
2 tablespoons flour
steamed rice

Chutney and sambals (condiments):
Major Grey chutney
crystallized ginger bits
grated coconut
currants
chopped nuts (almonds, pistachios, or pignoli)
chopped onion (scallions or red onions)
bacon crumbles

Season chicken with salt, pepper, and lemon pepper. Place in a roasting pan and bake about 90 minutes, until the juices run clear or until a meat thermometer inserted in thickest part of the thigh reaches 180* F. When chicken is cool enough to handle, remove skin, all bones and excess fat. Cut into large bite size pieces and set aside.

In heavy stockpot sauté onion, apple, and curry powder in ⅔ cup hot chicken fat until golden, but not brown. Remove onions and stir 2 tablespoons flour into bubbling, remaining fat and cook 3 minutes. Slowly stir chicken stock into flour mixture, blend while stirring. Add onions and chicken. Simmer slowly for 10 minutes, stirring frequently. Serve over steamed rice and serve condiments on the side.

Chicken Grandmere

1 (3 ½ pound) whole chicken
1 clove garlic, cut in half
salt
freshly ground black pepper
2 tablespoons butter
¼ cup cognac
1 med onion, chopped
½ pound fresh mushrooms, sliced
½ cup dry red wine
¼ cup dry white wine
1 cup chicken broth
1 tablespoon flour
1 tablespoon butter
¼ cup snipped parsley

Salt and pepper chicken all over, rub with the cut garlic, placing any remaining pieces inside the chicken. In Dutch oven or casserole, melt 2 tablespoons butter. When butter foams, place the chicken in the Dutch oven and brown all over. In a small saucepan, heat the cognac, pour it over the chicken and ignite. When flame dies, remove the chicken from the Dutch oven and set aside. Add chopped onion to the Dutch oven and sauté until golden. Add mushrooms and sauté for two minutes, stirring. Add the two wines and chicken broth and stir up brown bits that cling to the bottom of pan. Turn heat off. Knead the flour and butter together into a smooth ball. Over medium heat, blend it into the liquid in the pan until the sauce is smooth and comes to a boil. Lower the heat. Carve the chicken into serving pieces and return to the Dutch oven with the parsley. Cook in upper third of preheated 350° oven for about 50 minutes.

Chicken Tagine With Olives And Preserved Lemons

rock salt

1 whole large chicken, cut into 8 pieces

1 tablespoon white wine vinegar

5 tablespoons olive oil

1 large bunch fresh cilantro, chopped

1 teaspoon cinnamon

½ teaspoon real saffron

pinch fine salt

½ pound onions, chopped

5 cloves garlic, chopped

1 teaspoon cumin

1 teaspoon ground ginger

1 teaspoon paprika

1 teaspoon turmeric

¼ pound gizzards, optional

¼ pound chicken liver, optional

¼ cup mixed olives, pitted

3 small Preserved Lemons (*see recipe 263)

First rub the rock salt into the chicken pieces and then wash the chicken in the white wine vinegar and water. Leave for 10 minutes. Rinse and dry and place onto a clean plate. In a large bowl, mix the olive oil, coriander, cinnamon, saffron, fine salt, ½ the onions, garlic, cumin, ginger, paprika, and turmeric. Mix all these ingredients into the oil and crush the garlic and add a little water to make a paste. Roll the chicken pieces into the marinade and leave for 10 to 15 minutes. For cooking, use a tagine (traditional Moroccan dish) or a deep, heavy bottom casserole dish. Heat the dish and add 2 tablespoons of olive oil to the hot dish. Drop in the chicken and pour over the excess marinade juices. Add the remaining onions, gizzards,

chicken livers, olives, and chopped preserved lemons (no pulp). Cook in medium hot oven (350* F) for 45-60 minutes.
Serve with Bulgur Pilaf (*see recipe page 291).

Poulet En Papillote

4 skinless, boneless chicken breasts
4 pieces of Canadian bacon, thinly sliced

For the duxelles:
1 onion, chopped
1 shallot, chopped
4 ounce mushrooms
parsley
2 tablespoons butter

Sear the chicken breasts in a small amount of oil for about 2 minutes per side. Remove and keep warm. To prepare the duxelles, purée the onions, shallots, parsley and mushrooms in a food processor. Melt the butter in a skillet and add the mushroom mixture. Sauté until the mushroom mixture has lost most of its moisture. Place each chicken breast on a piece of foil. Top with 1 tablespoon of the duxelles; add a slice of bacon and then another tablespoon of the duxelles. Close foil tightly and bake for 25 minutes at 425°. To serve, remove the chicken from the foil packets and place on a warmed serving dish.

Mr. Glenn Stanley's Brissled Chicken

8 chicken halves
4 cups apple cider vinegar
4 cups water
½ tablespoons sugar
2 sticks butter
1 ½ tablespoons Worcestershire
salt to taste
red pepper to taste

Combine the vinegar, water, sugar, butter, Worcestershire, salt, and red pepper to taste in a large saucepan. Bring the mixture to a boil and remove from heat. Dip the chicken halves in sauce before placing on grill. Baste constantly, turning often. Keep fire low and cook slowly. Yield: 8 servings
Note: Ribs and pork chops are equally good prepared this way.

Chicken Piccata

4 chicken breasts, pounded thin
½ cup of olive oil
½ cup of flour
3 tablespoons of butter
½ cup of white wine
juice of 2 lemons
1 cup chicken broth
salt and freshly ground
pepper to taste

Dredge each chicken breast in flour to coat and shake off excess.
Heat oil in a large sauté pan set on medium heat. Place chicken breasts in pan and cook until lightly browned on both sides, about 2-3 minutes for each side. Drain the oil and add butter, wine, lemon, salt and freshly ground black pepper. Cook for 1 minute. Add the broth and cook until the liquid is reduced by half, 5 to 6 minutes (sprinkle a little flour in when it starts boiling to thicken.) Transfer chicken to serving dish, top with sauce and a slice of lemon for garnish. Yield: serves 4

Feta Chicken Breasts

6 boneless chicken breasts
2 tablespoons lemon juice
salt
freshly ground black pepper
4 ounces feta, crumbled
¼ cup red pepper, finely chopped
¼ cup parsley, chopped

Put chicken breasts in baking dish. Drizzle with 1 tablespoon lemon juice. Season with salt and freshly ground black pepper. Top with feta and drizzle with remaining 1 tablespoon lemon juice. Bake at 350° for 35 to 40 minutes, until cooked through. Sprinkle with red pepper and parsley before serving.

Coq au Vin

1 fryer, quartered and washed
¼ pound bacon cut in 1 inch strips
10 tablespoons butter, divided
salt and freshly ground pepper to taste
¼ cup cognac
4 cups burgundy, warmed
1 thyme bouquet garni
2 cloves garlic, mashed
1 tablespoons tomato paste
2 jars little white onions, sautéed
1 pound mushrooms, sautéed
3 tablespoons flour

Simmer bacon pieces 5 minutes in water to blanch (this reduces the fat in the bacon), then drain. In heavy pot, sauté the bacon in 3 tablespoons butter, remove to side dish. Brown the chicken over medium heat, add salt and freshly ground black pepper and bacon. Lower heat, cover and cook 10 minutes, turning once. Pour warmed cognac over, ignite. When flame subsides add warmed red wine, thyme bouquet garnish, garlic, and tomato paste. Lower heat, then cover and cook for 35 to 40 minutes. Remove chicken and place on serving dish. Arrange sautéed onions around chicken and keep warm. Bring liquid to a boil and cook until slightly reduced, correct seasonings, remove bouquet garni. Lower heat and simmer and beat in beurre manie (3 tablespoons flour and 3 tablespoons butter), add sautéed mushrooms. Pour sauce over chicken and serve.

Chicken Breasts with Dried Beef

4 boned chicken breasts
1 jar dried beef slices
1 cup sour cream
4 slices bacon, halved
2 tablespoons sherry
1 can cream of mushroom soup

Pound chicken breasts until flattened. Line bottom of casserole with slices of dried beef. Put slice of dried beef on portion of chicken breast. Roll breast up and wrap a half slice of bacon around each individual roll. Place these on top of the dried beef in the casserole. Mix soup, sour cream, and sherry and pour over the chicken rolls. Bake for 2 hours, uncovered, in 300°F oven, then for 20 minutes in 350°F oven. Good served with congealed fruit salad, wild rice, and green beans. Yield: 4

Goat Cheese Chicken Rolls

4 chicken breast halves
½ cup goat cheese
¼ cup sun-dried tomatoes
fresh chopped basil
fresh chopped garlic
1 cup white wine
¼ cup olive oil
2 tablespoons butter

Preheat oven to 425°. Flatten chicken breasts. Evenly layer cheese, tomatoes, basil, and garlic onto each breast. Roll each breast and secure with food loop or tie with string. Heat oil on med high and brown the rolls. Deglaze pan with wine, then reduce heat and whisk in butter, pour over rolls. Bake for 15 minutes at 425°.

Note: The ingenious silicone Food Loop makes stuffing, rolling and tying your food a cinch! No more fumbling with messy twine or toothpicks. The Food Loop keeps all of your fillings neatly tucked inside and your food securely wrapped.

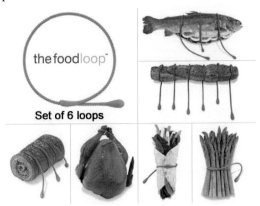

the foodloop
Set of 6 loops

http://www.thefoodloop.com

Jamaican Jerk Chicken

skinned chicken breasts or legs; do not debone breasts
soy sauce
¼ teaspoon Boston Jerk Seasoning per piece; if this Jamaican import is
    not available, make your own seasoning with recipe below

Rub breast or leg with jerk seasoning. Place in plastic bag with soy sauce and marinade for four hours or overnight, Cook on grill for one hour, turn basting after 30 minutes. I either use imported Jamaican jerk sauce or make my own:

Jamaican Jerk Seasoning:
½ cup ground allspice
½ cup brown sugar (add more if desired)
8 cloves garlic
6 scotch bonnet peppers or equivalent; add seeds and all
2 bunches scallions
1 teaspoon cinnamon
1 tablespoon ground thyme or some fresh
½ teaspoon nutmeg
2 tablespoons soy sauce (enough to make paste)

Put everything in food processor and blend until smooth. This will keep indefinitely in the refrigerator. Adjust amount of peppers to taste.

Chicken Cordon Bleu

8 boneless chicken breasts
4 slices prosciutto
4 slices provolone cheese
Kitchen Bouquet
salt
freshly ground black pepper
flour
1 can cream of mushroom soup
½ pint sour cream
½ cup dry white wine
oil for frying

Pound chicken very thin. Put slice of prosciutto and cheese on chicken. Top with another piece of chicken, again pounding to flatten. Brush with Kitchen Bouquet, sprinkle with salt and freshly ground black pepper. Dust lightly with flour. Heat oil in small pan and brown them one or two at a time and place them in a baking dish. Drain off most of the oil. Add can of soup, stirring and scraping the bottom and sides. Pour this over rolls and bake for 30 minutes at 350°, then reduce heat and bake 15 minutes more at 300°, covered with foil. Remove chicken to a platter and keep warm. Next blend wine and sour cream in the baking dish and cook 15 minutes at 300°. Before serving, taste gravy and adjust salt and freshly ground black pepper.

Rum Point Chicken in Coconuts

6 coconuts
2 cups chicken, cooked and cubed
1 carrot, cut into 2 inch pieces
1 onion, quartered
6 sprigs of parsley
1 tsp salt
⅔ cup butter
⅔ cups flour
4 cups chicken broth
2 cups cream
1 egg yolk
salt to taste
freshly ground black pepper to taste
dash of nutmeg
Tabasco
2 small cans pimiento, chopped
sherry to taste
1 loaf of unsliced bread

Cut tops from coconuts and save. Wash inside of coconuts and prop shells in water-filled oven pan (approx ½ way up coconuts). Cook chicken in water seasoned with the carrots, onion, salt and 6 sprigs parsley. Let chicken cool in its own broth before skinning, deboning and cutting into large bite size pieces. To prepare chicken a la king: melt butter, add flour, and cook until flour taste is gone, 1 or 2 minutes. Add heated chicken broth and cream, whisk over low heat until thickened and smooth. Add egg yolk gradually and stir for 1 minute. Add salt and freshly ground black pepper, nutmeg, and Tabasco to taste. Add 2 cups of cubed stewed chicken and pimiento. Fill coconuts ¾ full and glue tops on coconuts with a paste made of flour and water. Bake at least 2 hours in 350° oven in pan of water (cook longer if possible; it improves flavor). To make bread stands for coconuts, cut 1 inch thick slices of bread from an unsliced loaf. Cut a round hole in middle of each slice. Toast the bread stands and prop coconuts up in these. Cover toast with chopped parsley. Serve with fluffy rice and fruit salad. Extra chicken a la king can be frozen for later use.

The Phantom Cook's Cold Chicken Roulade

1 chicken, about 3 pounds
salt and freshly ground black pepper
¼ pound ham slices
⅓ cup bread crumbs, toasted
¼ cup parsley, minced
4 ounces black olives, sliced
1 teaspoon oregano
¼ pound salami, sliced
3 eggs, hard cooked and shelled
6–8 slices bacon

Carefully debone chicken by cutting down the back bone, leaving wings in place (keep skin intact after incising back - reserve bones and giblets for stock). Place chicken skin side down on a piece of plastic wrap and spread meat around to form as even a layer as possible. Sprinkle lightly with salt and freshly ground black pepper, than place ham slices evenly over chicken. Combine breadcrumbs, parsley, and oregano; sprinkle ham slices with half this mixture. Sprinkle olives over all and place salami slices on top. Sprinkle with remaining crumbs and place eggs in a row in the center. Fold chicken tightly around the eggs using the plastic wrap as an aid. Carefully remove the plastic wrap and tie the roulades at 1 inch-intervals and arrange bacon slices on top. Bake, seam side down, at 350º for about 50 minutes, basting often. Remove bacon slices, turn heat to 425º and continue to bake another 10 minutes or until golden brown. Remove from oven and place on a serving dish to cool, then refrigerate overnight. Serve in slices on a platter lined with greens and vegetable julienne. This presentation is sensational and is perfect for an al fresco luncheon or a picnic. Serve with Anchovy Dipping Sauce (*see recipe page 268). Yield: serves 6 – 8.
Contributor: Bettie McGowin Miller-The Phantom Cook

Chicken Livers in Red Wine

2 pounds chicken livers
9 tablespoons butter
2 bell peppers, chopped
½ pound mushrooms
½ cup red wine
1 bay leaf
salt
freshly ground black pepper
hot buttered toast

Sauté the mushrooms and chopped bell peppers in 3 tablespoons butter for 3 minutes. In another pan sauté the chicken livers in 6 tablespoons butter for 2 minutes. Combine the mushroom and liver mixtures, add ½ cup red wine, bay leaf, salt and freshly ground black pepper to taste. Simmer the mixture for 10 minutes. Serve on hot buttered toast.

Stonewall Chicken Livers

1 pound chicken livers
1 cup chicken stock
¼ pound mushrooms
water to thin
1 tablespoons flour
1 teaspoon curry

Sauté mushrooms in butter. Add washed and dried chicken livers, sauté until brown and crisp. Mix flour, curry, chicken stock and the juice from the mushrooms (if canned) and shake over the mushrooms and livers. Add water if sauce is too thick. Serve over brown rice.

Elmira's Turkey

1 turkey
1 quart water
salt
freshly ground black pepper
flour
butter

Season turkey with salt and pepper. Place turkey in steamer insert pan, with hot water in bottom pan. Cover tightly with lid. Cook in 300° oven until meat thermometer reaches about 145°. Remove lid. Mix flour and water and dab over turkey and continue cooking until temperature reaches 165-175°. If not well browned, turn the broiler on for a minute or two, watching carefully as it browns.
Note: Elmira never prepared a dry turkey. She insisted on steaming her holiday birds before their final roast!

Brine for Turkey

1 cup brown sugar
1 cup salt
6–8 juniper berries
½ cup brandy
1 gallon water
1 orange, juiced and peeled
1 lemon, juiced and peeled

Mix all ingredients. Place in turkey bag or large pot. Marinate 24 hours before roasting turkey. **Regardless of the method you use to cook your holiday bird, plan to place it in a brine bath overnight before it goes into the oven or on the grill. Brining enhances the flavor and makes it moist

To Brown a Turkey

1 egg, beaten
2 teaspoons milk

Beat egg with a little milk and brush turkey. Turn heat up to 450° and watch it brown. Only takes 3 to 5 minutes.

Turkey Chili

4 tablespoons olive oil

10 garlic cloves, minced

4 medium onions, minced

5 celery stalks with tops, finely chopped

3 red, yellow, or green bell peppers, cored, seeded, and diced

4 tablespoons tomato paste

2 ½ pounds ground turkey

½ cup Dijon mustard

½ cup fresh basil or 1 tablespoon dried

3 tablespoons ground cumin

1 tablespoon dried oregano

5 tablespoons chili powder

2 to 3 bay leaves

2 cups dry red wine

⅛ to ¼ teaspoon cayenne

1 tablespoon molasses

1 (16 oz) can pinto beans, drained and rinsed

1 (16 oz) can navy beans, drained and rinsed

1 (16 oz) can kidney beans, drained and rinsed

6 cups (two 28 ounce cans) crushed tomatoes

1 cup chopped fresh tomato

2 cups beer, preferably dark

salt and freshly ground black pepper

¾ cup chopped Italian parsley

In a large, heavy-bottomed pot, heat the oil over medium heat. Add the garlic and sauté until golden, about 4 minutes. Add the onions, celery, and peppers; cook until the vegetables are soft, about 5 minutes. Add the tomato paste, stir to combine, and cook 2 minutes. Add the chicken or chicken-turkey mixture and sauté, stirring to keep the meat from clumping together, until cooked through, about 7 minutes. Stir in the mustard, basil, cumin, oregano, chili powder, bay leaves, wine, and cayenne. Add the molasses, beans, and tomatoes. Stir in 1 cup of the beer, reduce the heat, and simmer 1 hour, stirring occasionally. Season the chili to taste with the salt and freshly ground black pepper. Add the remaining beer if necessary to thin. Add the parsley, stir thoroughly, and cook 5 minutes. Remove the bay leaves and serve with the suggested garnishes.

Jack Stallworth's Turkey

2 large brown paper bags (use double thickness)
1 turkey
2 med onions
3 sprigs parsley
2 stalks celery, cut into pieces
¼ bell pepper
olive oil or safflower oil
salt
freshly ground black pepper
egg (optional)
milk (optional)

Set oven to 300°. Wash turkey and dry thoroughly with paper towels (this is important so the moisture will not deteriorate the bag). Brush salt and pepper inside and outside, rub the bird well with olive or safflower oil. Do the same with double shopping bags. No spot should be left without oil. Stuff the cavity of the bird with the vegetables-then slip the turkey into the oiled bag, fold the ends over tightly and staple it well. Place in a baking pan and bake for 15 minutes lb for a 12 to 14 pound bird or 12 minutes/lb for a large bird. Most of the time the bird will be golden brown. If it isn't brown enough, pat the oil off the bird and brush over with an egg beaten and a little milk. Turn up the heat to 450° and watch it brown. It takes only 3 to 5 minutes. Results - juicy brown bird. Note: Allow turkey to sit at room temp for about 3 hours before roasting.

Romertorf Quail

4 quail
½ cup chicken broth
½ teaspoon salt
freshly ground pepper
1 cup red wine
2 slices bacon
dash of thyme
½ lb mushrooms, quartered if large
1 onion, quartered

Soak clay pot 10 minutes. Put bacon slices in bottom of pot. Salt and pepper quail. Place on top of bacon. Sprinkle with thyme. Add mushrooms and onions. Mix chicken broth and wine and pour over quail. Put lid on pot. Put in cold oven, then set oven at 450 ° and cook for 1 hour. Lift birds from pot and place on heated platter. Whisk in beurre manie (beurre manié is a paste of flour and softened butter, usually in equal parts, used to thicken sauces). Return to oven, uncovered for 10 minutes to thicken gravy.
Suggested accompaniment: cheese grits and biscuits.

Pheasant With Wild Mushrooms

2 whole pheasants, or 4 pheasant breasts, boned, wings still attached
1 stick butter, softened
1 tablespoon finely chopped garlic
2 tablespoons finely chopped flat leaf parsley, leaves only
2 leeks, light part only, well washed; and chopped coarsely
⅔ cup chardonnay
1 pint heavy cream
8 ounce porcini or shiitake mushrooms, sliced
1 stick butter

The night before cooking, dissolve a cup of salt into a gallon of water; put the brine and the pheasant into a large plastic food storage bag (those turkey roasting bags are perfect). Marinate the birds overnight, refrigerated. Rinse the pheasants very well and pat dry. Season the pheasant with a little salt and pepper. Combine the softened butter with the garlic and parsley. Cut slits in the loose parts of the pheasant's skin, and insert pats of the herb butter under the skin, reserving about 2 Tbsps of the herb butter for later. Preheat the oven to 450*. Place the pheasant's breast-side-down on a roasting pan. When the oven reaches 450*, lower the temperature to 375*, and put the pheasant in the middle of the oven (If you have a convection oven, turn the convection feature on). Roast the pheasants for 20 minutes. Turn the heat in the oven back up to 450*, and continue roasting another 10-15 minutes, until a meat thermometer inserted into the meat of the thigh reads 170º. (If using breasts take them out at 160*.) While the birds are in the oven, heat the herb butter in a skillet over medium heat. Add the leeks and sauté until soft. Add the wine and reduce by half. Add the mushrooms and cook until soft. Add the cream and reduce until it thickens. Add salt and pepper to taste. Let the pheasant rest for about five minutes after taking it out of the oven. Slice the breast meat it ¼ inch thick on the bias. Place he leek sauce on the plate and fan the pheasant slices out over it. Arrange he mushrooms on the plate. Yield: Serves four.

Apricot Glazed Cornish Hens

6 Cornish hens
½ cup Riesling wine
½ cup chicken broth
salt
1/2 teaspoon thyme
freshly ground pepper
1 (6 oz) jar apricot preserves
6 slices ginger, cut ⅛ thick
1 tablespoons sugar
1 tablespoons lemon juice
½ stick butter
1 large onion, slice thin

Season hens inside and out with salt and freshly ground black pepper. Place a slice of ginger in each hen. Fold wings back and tie legs together. Melt butter and brush each hen with butter, then with apricot preserves. Scatter onions in large roasting pan; pour broth and wine into pan. Sprinkle thyme over ingredients in pan. Place hens in pan and roast in preheated 375° oven for 1 hour or until hens are golden and tender. Transfer to platter.

Roasted Cornish Hens

2 Cornish hens
Asian olive oil
salt
freshly ground pepper
1 tablespoons orange marmalade
¼ teaspoon lime juice

Wash hens and dry with paper towel. Rub with Asian oil (preferably a few hours ahead). Salt and freshly ground black pepper hens inside and out. Roast on upright roasters or small cans at 350° for an hour, then mix marmalade and lime juice and brush on birds and continue to roast for 30 minutes.
*Good served with wild rice with onions and almonds and pears baked with chutney!

Roasted Duck

1 (5 lb) duck
1 tsp soda
1 potato, quartered
½ onion
water
1 apple, quartered
1 sprig celery leaves
1 orange
¼ onion
1 strip bacon
cognac or Grand Marnier
salt
red pepper
black pepper

Cover duck with heavily salted water to which 1 tsp. soda added. Soak for 1 hour. Rinse and place in pan of fresh water with ½ onion and quartered potato. Boil gently for 30 to 45 minutes. Drain and wash. Season cavity with salt, red and black pepper. Insert ¼ onion, apple, and celery leaves in cavity. Place duck in roaster in 1 inch of water. Squeeze orange over duck, lay strip of bacon over breast. Salt and pepper outside. Cook, covered at 275 ° for 4 hours, basting every 30 minutes. Cook uncovered for the last 30 minutes to brown, turning oven to broil the last few minutes. Brush with cognac or Grand Marnier during the last few minutes of browning.

Choose Your Bird Carefully

All men possess bird qualities
When seeking a mate carefully look at his bird side
Turkeys are harmless, but proud and inconsiderate
Buzzards are scavengers and tear you apart
Vampires suck and go for blood
Owls are wise and usually reserved
Bats are night creatures
Eagles are brave and carry you high
Hawks will seize and possess you
Wrens are benign and offer sweet serenades
Pheasants beat their wings and keep you away
Peacocks are vain and demand attention
Didappers flit in and flit out
Go forth forewarned…

Meats

Beef en Gelee

 beef tenderloin
 envelopes gelatin
 cans consommé
½ cup white wine
 carrot, slightly cook
fresh mushrooms

Cook filet in 425° oven 9 minutes per pound for medium rare. Refrigerate overnight. Slice into ¼ inch slices and set aside. Soften gelatin in consommé; bring to a quick boil, stirring constantly. Remove from heat and stir in wine. Pour a thin layer of consommé into platter; chill until set. Arrange carrot and mushroom slices on gelatin, cover with a thin layer of consommé mixture. Arrange beef slices in center of gelatin, forming into original tenderloin shape. Spoon remaining mixture over beef to form a light glaze. Chill thoroughly. Good dish for a summer buffet!

Chateaubriand Marchand de Vin

chateaubriands, about ½ pound each per guest
melted butter, enough to baste chateaubriands during cooking
beef marrow

For sauce:
⅔ cup of finely chopped green onions
¼ pound butter
1 cup red wine (preferably good Bordeaux)
dash of cognac
juice of 1 lemon
chopped parsley

Prepare beef: Sear the chateaubriands, about 2 minutes per side on a hot grill. Season with salt and pepper and roast in a 425° for about 12 minutes or until internal temperature 120° for rare. During the cooking, brush them frequently with melted butter and turn them often. Meanwhile, extract the marrow and slice it in thin rounds. Poach these for about 1 minute in boiling salted water. Prepare sauce: Sauté green onions in ¼ pound butter until just colored. Add red wine and cook this down to one half its volume. Add cognac, pat of butter and the lemon. Sprinkle the sauce heavily with parsley. When the meat is done, remove it to hot plates, pour the sauce over each portion and top with slices of poached marrow.
*Be careful not to overcook!! Internal temp of 120° for rare, 130° for medium rare.

Filet of Beef Duke of Wellington

1 (3-4 pound) beef tenderloin
½ cup butter
salt
freshly ground black pepper
¼ cup pâté de foie gras
6 ounces pâté de foie gras
6 mushrooms, chop fine
1 egg, beaten
1 cup veal stock
2 tablespoons red wine
1 package pie crust mix (2 crusts) or pate brisee II (*see recipe page 327)

Trim fat from beef tenderloin; cover generously with butter and sprinkle with salt and freshly ground black pepper. Use a butcher's steel and make a tunnel through filet lengthwise. Stuff incision with 6 ounces of pâté de foie gras and chopped mushrooms. Sauté 4 minutes on each side; remove, drain and chill.

Prepare piecrust and roll out ⅛ inch thick. Spread crust with extra pâté and mushrooms. Place beef on crust and fold dough over to cover it completely. Trim off extra dough and set it aside. Seal edges with beaten egg. Place on baking sheet, seam side down. Cut designs from reserved crust and place on top of roll. Brush with beaten egg. Bake in a 425° oven for 15 to 20 minutes or until browned. Add veal stock to pan drippings. Add ¼ cup pâté, chopped mushrooms and red wine. Simmer until sauce thickens. Slice beef and serve with sauce.

Individual Beef Wellingtons with Green Peppercorn Sauce

4 filets
2 strips bacon
2 teaspoons salt
2 ½ teaspoons freshly ground pepper
1 tablespoon butter, clarified
1/4 cup cognac
2 tablespoons heavy cream
3 tablespoons green peppercorns (water packed), drained
1 (8 ounce) tin pâté de foie gras
1 recipe Pate Brisee II
1 egg yolk
½ cup heavy cream

Pat filets dry and sprinkle each with ¼ teaspoon freshly ground black pepper and ½ teaspoon salt, pressing seasoning into meat. Wrap each filet with ½ strip bacon. Sear steaks in clarified butter 1 ½ minutes per side, transfer with slotted spoon to plate and cool. Pour out all but 1 tablespoon fat, add cognac and deglaze skillet. Cook over moderate heat until reduced to approximately 1 tablespoon. Then add the cream, 1 tablespoon green peppercorns; and the remaining 1 ½ teaspoons freshly ground pepper. Reduce to approximately ⅓ cup. Transfer to saucepan. Wrap steaks in Saran wrap and chill for 1 hour.

In small bowl, combine the pâté and the remaining 2 tablespoons green peppercorns, crushing slightly. Chill (covered) for 30 minutes.

Roll dough into rectangle ⅛ inch thick. Discard bacon and string and spread pate mixture on each side of steak. Cut out 4 rectangles of dough. Put steak, pâté side down, in center of rectangle and fold dough to make packages, moisten with water to seal edges. Place seam side down on baking sheet. Form dough into ball, roll out on floured surface and cut into decorative shapes. Brush shapes with water and divide among packages. Chill, covered loosely with Saran wrap for 1 to 4 hours. Make a ¼ inch hole in top of each package for a steam vent, brush with egg wash (egg yolk plus 2 tablespoons heavy cream) and bake in 450° oven 25 to 30 minutes or until golden. Transfer carefully to heated platter. Heat sauce until hot and spoon over Beef Wellingtons.

Pesto Meatloaf

1 spicy uncooked pork sausage
olive oil
1 onion, finely chopped
8 ounce package mushrooms, finely chopped
salt and freshly ground pepper to taste
1 egg, beaten
½ cup seasoned dry bread crumbs
½ cup prepared pesto
½ pound lean ground beef
½ pound lean ground pork

Preheat oven to 375º. Remove casing from pork sausage, crumble sausage and set aside. In a large skillet, heat olive oil and add onion and mushrooms. Sauté until vegetables are tender and liquid has evaporated, about 15 minutes. Place in large bowl and let cool 15 minutes. Add salt, freshly ground black pepper, beaten egg, bread crumbs, and pesto. Mix well. Then add ground beef, ground pork, and reserved sausage. Mix gently but thoroughly until combined. Form meat mixture into a loaf and place in a shallow roasting pan. Bake at 375º for 60-75 minutes, or until internal temperature registers 160º. Let stand 15 minutes before slicing.
Serves 4-6
Note: Slice leftovers to make a delightful sandwich the next day!

Slow Cooked Pot Roast

1 (5 lb) beef roast
paprika
olive oil
3 red bell peppers, cut into strips
2 medium onions, quartered
1 carrot, cut into chunks
6 cloves garlic
1 small can tomato sauce
1 glass red wine
1 hot pepper
salt
freshly ground black pepper

Roll roast in paprika and sear in olive oil. Sauté the peppers in skillet. Add them to the meat along with the vegetables. Pour the wine and tomato sauce into the skillet and cook down to thicken a bit. Pour mixture over the roast. Grind on some freshly ground black pepper and a sprinkle of salt. Cook in a slow 300° oven for 3 to 5 hours. When meat is done, push vegetables through a sieve to create a puree or gravy (do not use blender).

Steak Diane

2 (6 oz) filet mignons
⅛ teaspoon salt
⅛ teaspoon freshly ground pepper
2 tablespoons butter
1 teaspoon Dijon-style mustard
2 tablespoons shallots, minced
1 tablespoon butter
1 tablespoon lemon juice
1 ½ teaspoon Worcestershire sauce
1 tablespoon fresh chives, minced
1 teaspoon brandy
1 tablespoons fresh parsley, minced

Season both sides of steak with salt and freshly ground pepper. Melt butter in a heavy skillet; add mustard and shallots. Sauté over medium heat 1 minute. Add steaks and cook approximately 4 minutes on each side for medium-rare. Remove steaks to serving plate and keep warm. Add to pan drippings, 1 tablespoon butter, lemon juice, Worcestershire sauce and chives. Cook for 2 minutes. Add brandy; pour sauce over steaks. Sprinkle parsley over the top.

Filet Mignon Marsala

4 filets
salt
freshly ground pepper
2 tablespoons butter
½ cup dry Marsala wine
1 clove garlic, minced
1 tablespoon cornstarch
½ cup beef broth
2 scallions, sliced

Sauté scallions and garlic lightly in butter. Pour in Marsala and cook over medium heat. Combine corn starch with beef broth. Stir into pan, cook, stirring constantly until gravy boils 2 minutes. Season with salt and freshly ground black pepper as desired. Keep warm. Broil or grill filets to desired doneness. (internal temperature of 120° for rare or 130° for medium rare). Serve over broiled steaks. Serves 2

Choucroute Garnie

2 pounds sauerkraut
salt
2 slices bacon, chopped
1 cup finely chopped onion
1 teaspoon chopped garlic
1 bay leaf
6 juniper berries, crushed
freshly ground pepper
1 ham steak
1 polish sausage, prick with tines of fork
8 slices roast pork
½ teaspoon caraway seeds
½ cup dry white wine
½ cup chicken broth

If you like sauerkraut that is relatively sour, do not rinse it, but simply squeeze it dry. If you like it less sour, run it under cold water and drain in a colander. Press to extract excess moisture.

Heat the bacon in a casserole or Dutch oven and cook until rendered of fat. Pour off excess fat. Add the onion and garlic and cook until onion is wilted. Add the sauerkraut. Tie the bay leaf, juniper berries, and caraway seed in cheese cloth and add to pot. Add the wine, chicken broth, salt and freshly ground black pepper to taste and bring to a boil. Arrange the pork, ham and sausage over the kraut. Cover closely and cook 1 hour. Discard cheesecloth bag.

Onion-Mustard Roast Pork Loin

1 4 lb pork loin roast
1 cup prepared mustard
2 cups onion, chopped fine
freshly ground black pepper
salt

Make several cuts in roast and season thoroughly being sure to get seasoning into cuts as well as on sides. Spread onions and mustard over roast sides. Place roast in an uncovered pan, fat side up with small amount water. Insert meat thermometer and bake at 350° F about 2 ½ hours thermometer reaches 185°. Source: Blue Moon Inn

Andouille-Stuffed Pork Tenderloin

2 large pork tenderloins (about 4 pounds each)
1 tablespoon olive oil

Andouille stuffing:
2 tablespoons butter
2 ½ cups chopped onions
½ cup chopped celery
1 cup chopped bell pepper
1 pound chopped andouille
2 tablespoons butter
1 tablespoon chopped garlic
1 teaspoon Tabasco
1 cup chicken stock
¾ cup fresh bread crumbs, very fine

Roasted garlic-rosemary glaze:
3 tablespoons softened butter
2 cloves garlic
½ teaspoon garlic, chopped
2 ounces highly reduced veal stock or demi-glace
½ tsp fresh rosemary, chopped

1. Melt the 2 tablespoon butter in a large skillet over high heat. Add half each of the onions, celery, and bell pepper, and sauté until lightly browned.
2. Add the remaining onions, celery, and bell pepper, along with the andouille, butter, and Tabasco. Sauté about three minutes.
3. Add the chicken stock and bring to a boil. Reduce to a simmer and cook until most of the fat rises to the surface; skim this off, and cook until all the

liquid has been absorbed, but the mixture is still moist.

4. Stir in the bread crumbs to combine completely. Turn the mixture out onto a sheet pan to cool.

5. With knife-sharpening steel or the handle of a wooden spoon, push a hole into the large end of the pork tenderloin, going in as deep as you can. Pack this hole with the cooled stuffing. (You will be surprised how much the meat will stretch, and how much stuffing will fit, but it does take a little patience.)

6. Heat up a grill or a large iron skillet, and sear the outside of the stuffed tenderloins. Do not cook through yet. You can prepare the dish up to this point and hold it in the refrigerator for later use the same day (In fact, this helps the stuffing to set).

7. To finish the stuffed pork, slice the tenderloin into discs about three-fourths inch thick. Coat lightly with flour, salt, and freshly ground black pepper.

8. Heat the olive oil in a skillet on top of the stove and add the pork discs. Put the skillet into a preheated 400° oven, and cook until medium--about six minutes--turning once.

9. Make the glaze in the skillet in which the pork was roasted. Melt 1 tablespoon of the butter, and sauté the garlic and rosemary for about two minutes. Add the veal stock or demi-glace. Bring to a boil, remove from the heat. Whisk in the remainder of the butter to create an emulsified sauce.

Yield: serves four to six

Pork Chops in Caper Sauce

4 large pork chops
1 tablespoon flour
salt
freshly ground black pepper
1 (16 oz) can beef broth
1 tablespoon Dijon mustard
1 tablespoon capers
1 tablespoon sour cream

Combine flour, salt, and freshly ground black pepper. Dredge chops in flour mixture and sauté over medium-high heat until browned on both sides (approximately 2 minutes per side). Remove chops from skillet, and turn heat to medium low. Add broth and stir in mustard and capers. Cook 5 minutes. Return chops to skillet, cover and cook for 45-60 minutes. Before serving, stir sour cream (optional) into sauce. Yield: 4 servings

Elmira's Cabbage Rolls

1 large head cabbage
2 pounds ground beef
1 pound ground pork
4 onions, chopped
1 bunch celery, chopped
2 cloves garlic, minced
1 cup raw rice
salt
freshly ground pepper
Lemon Pepper Marinade
1 large can or jar sauerkraut
1 large can tomatoes
6 strips bacon

Wilt cabbage by placing cored head in large kettle with water; steam, removing leaves as they wilt. Place strips of bacon on bottom of roaster (one with a cover). Mix meats, onion, celery, garlic, and raw rice. Season to taste with salt, freshly ground black pepper and lemon pepper marinade. Make rolls by placing about ½ cup of mixture in each leaf and wrapping. Place seam side down on bacon strips. Add just enough water to the pan so that the rolls will not stick while cooking. Simmer on top of stove, covered 1 or 2 hours. Cover with tomatoes and sauerkraut and continue to cook for another hour. Serve with a bowl of mashed potatoes! Serves 8
Note: Cabbage rolls are my favorite winter dish. They freeze well. I make them with the first frost (or in the Deep South when it drops below 60°) and stock my freezer. After freezing, add a little fresh sauerkraut before serving.

Tom Roberts' Stuffed Pork Tenderloin

1 (4 lb) pork tenderloin
salt
white pepper
2 boxes spinach; thaw and squeeze liquid out
2 tablespoons basil
1 tablespoon minced garlic
1 cup stone ground brown bread crumbs
1 egg
2 tablespoons olive oil
¼ cup Balsamic vinegar
¼ cup white wine
2 tablespoons parsley
2 ounces toasted pine nuts
tarragon (optional)

Carefully cut loin in spiral fashion starting with ¾ slash along length to create a rectangular sheet. Mix all ingredients to prepare filling. Salt and pepper pork, brush with olive oil.

Spread filling over rectangular pork, sprinkle with tarragon and roll like a jelly roll. Tie rolled loin at intervals, using food loops (www.foodloops. com) if available. Let it sit in refrigerator overnight. Start in hot oven (450º) to brown. After 10 or 15 minutes, reduce temperature to 350º and roast for about 1½ hours. Serves 8-10.

Note: You can carefully pierce small pork tenders with a butcher's steel, stuff them and bake. Slice 1/4 inch thick for appetizers!

Tom Roberts' Stuffed Pork Tenderloin

Medallions of Pork

3 pork tenderloins cut into ½ inch slices
2 teaspoons dry mustard
1 teaspoon salt
¼ teaspoon ground pepper
2 tablespoons butter
1 tablespoon flour
2 tablespoons water
minced parsley
zest of orange
parsley sprigs
2 cloves garlic, minced
orange slices
½ cup dry vermouth
½ cup white wine
¾ cup orange juice

Trim fat and sinew from loins and cut into ½ inch thick slices. Combine mustard, salt, and freshly ground black pepper and lightly rub into meat. In a large, heavy skillet, melt butter over medium-high heat and add pork slices and brown meat from 3 to 5 minutes on each side. Add vermouth, wine, minced garlic and juice; reduce heat. Simmer for 8 to 10 minutes until meat is tender. Remove medallions to a warm plate and cover. Make a paste of the flour and water. With a wire whisk, stir paste into pan juices and simmer to thicken gravy. When ready to serve, return medallions to hot pan for a minute; then arrange on a warm serving platter; cover with gravy. Sprinkle with minced parsley and zest of orange rind; place a sprig of parsley and slices of oranges around the plate. Yield: 6 servings
Note: Serve with buttered noodles, green vegetable, and spinach salad with mandarin oranges, toasted almonds, and poppy seed dressing.

Sauerkraut and Pork

4 pounds boneless pork shoulder, butt, or blade roast, trimmed

2 teaspoons paprika

1 teaspoon sea salt

freshly ground pepper

½ teaspoon dried sage

½ teaspoon dried thyme

¼ teaspoon dry mustard

2 tablespoons olive oil

3½ cups cabbage, shredded

2 cups onions, thinly sliced

½ cup carrots, diced

2 cloves garlic, minced

1 pound sauerkraut, rinsed and drained

1 cup chicken stock

12 fluid ounces beer

1 teaspoon caraway seeds

1 teaspoon dried savory

2 bay leaves

cooked spaetzle, for accompaniment

Combine paprika, sea salt, freshly ground black pepper, sage, thyme, and dry mustard. Rub blended spices over the pork, and marinate in the refrigerator for 4 hours or overnight. Heat the olive oil over medium heat in a large, heavy pot with a tight-fitting lid. Brown the meat on all sides. Remove meat from pan and pour out all but 2 tablespoons of fat. Add the cabbage, onions, carrots, stirring occasionally, until softened. Add garlic; cook until aromatic, about one minute. Add the sauerkraut, stock, beer, caraway seeds, savory, and bay leaves. Bring to a boil. Return the meat to the pot and cover. Braise in a 325° F oven for 2 hours, or until fork-tender;

check after one hour, and add additional stock, as necessary. When meat is cooked, remove the roast to a warm platter to rest. Skim off fat from juices in the pan. Slice roast, and arrange meat, vegetables, and juices in a covered dish to keep warm. Serve meat with vegetables, pan juices, and spaetzle.

Edna Mae's Barbecued Ribs

2 pounds small, lean pork ribs, trimmed of all fat
Lawry's seasoned salt
Cattlemen's or BBQ sauce of choice

Sprinkle ribs on both sides liberally with seasoned salt. Place ribs in roasting pan, meaty side up, in 350° oven and roast for approximately 1 ½ hours (do not let them dry out). Ribs can be prepared ahead to this point, then refrigerated or frozen. Allow ribs to come to room temp, if time allows, before placing on grill. Place on grill and brush with barbecue sauce. When ribs begin to brown, brush again with sauce before turning to brown other side. Do not overcook. Yield: 4 servings
Note: Serve with Better Baked Beans (*see recipe 225), potato salad, herbed tomatoes, and garlic bread.

Slow-Oven-Cooked Ribs

1 slab baby back ribs
garlic powder
Tony Cachere's Creole seasoning
liquid smoke flavoring

Rub ribs generously with Tony's seasoning and garlic powder. Pour about a tablespoon of liquid smoke and rub it in by hand. Wrap with aluminum foil and refrigerate overnight. The next morning, preheat oven to 225°, place ribs in foil in pan and cook for 8 hours. Carefully remove ribs from foil and place on grill for 10 to 45 minutes. Ribs should be prepared the night before cooking.

Tom Fitzmorris' Pork Loin

4 pounds pork tenderloin, 10-12 inches long, trimmed of fat and silver skin
¼ cup soy sauce
¼ cup freshly ground black pepper
salt

Sauce:

¼ cup fig preserves
⅓ cup orange marmalade (or substitute other kinds of jellies or preserves)
1 tablespoon Soy sauce
2 tablespoons tabasco, Caribbean-style steak sauce (or Pickapeppa)
¼ teaspoon salt

1. If cooking outside, build a fire with some wood chips or other smoking fuel in the pit. If cooking indoors, preheat the broiler and pan with the pan six inches from the heat.
2. Cut the pork loin from end to end into two pieces of the same size. Pour the ¼ cup soy sauce over the loins and coat them all over. Sprinkle on a bit of salt and the freshly ground black pepper. The freshly ground black pepper should create a distinct crust.
3. Place the loins as far away from the fire as possible, preferably near the smoke vent. The meat should not be directly above the fire. Close the cover and smoke at about 250° for three to four hours, until the interior temperature reaches 160° on a meat thermometer.
4. If using the oven, place the loins under the broiler and broil, turning once, for 10 minutes, until the exterior is well browned. Lower the heat to 275° and continue to cook until the interior temperature reaches 160°F on a meat thermometer. In either case, remove when the pork is cooked. Wrap in foil and refrigerate.

5. An hour or two before serving, slice the loins as thinly as you possibly can. (Having them cold will make that easier.) Line up the slices on a serving tray.

6. Combine all the sauce ingredients and serve with the pork.

Yield: serves about 20

Roast Loin of Pork

1 (6 lb) pork loin, trimmed
3 teaspoon salt
1 teaspoon thyme
1 teaspoon freshly ground black pepper
2 carrots, peeled and sliced
2 onions, peeled and divided
celery leaves
4 whole cloves
3 bay leaves
½ teaspoon ground nutmeg
2 cloves garlic, crushed
parsley
1 ¼ cups dry white wine
1 ¼ cups beef consommé
½ cup water

Season roast by rubbing with a mixture of salt, thyme, freshly ground black pepper. Place roast in a roasting pan and add vegetables, herbs and spices. Combine ½ cup wine and ½ cup consommé and pour over roast. More wine and consommé later if needed. Do not let the roast dry out, place uncovered in preheated 475° oven and roast 20 minutes. Reduce to 350° and roast covered about 35 minutes per pound or until meat meter registers well done. Remove roast and vegetables from pan. Save pan juices and mix with remaining wine and consommé and ½ cup water, scraping bottom of pan. Cook until slightly thick. Serve as gravy for roast.

Pork Chops-Bourbon Marinade

4 pork chops
2 tablesoons brown sugar
¼ cup soy sauce
¼ cup bourbon

Mix soy, bourbon, and sugar. Marinate chops 2 hours or more. Grill or bake at 325° for 1 hour, basting every 10 minutes.

Scaloppini al Limone

thin slices veal
teaspoon salt
reshly ground pepper
Worcestershire to taste
cup fresh cracker crumbs, finely crushed
emon pepper to taste
½ stick butter
thin lemon slices
¼ cup dry vermouth
hopped parsley

ound veal that has been salted, peppered and lightly sprinkled with
Worcestershire sauce. Pat cracker crumbs into meat. Melt butter in
onstick skillet and add lemon slices. Gently sauté veal, 4 or 5 minutes
ach side. Remove to warm platter and garnish with fresh parsley. Add
ermouth to skillet. Simmer until reduced by half and pour over veal.
ield: 4 servings

Osso Buco

6 meaty veal shanks, about 1 pound each
2 cups veal demi-glace
½ cup flour
1 teaspoon salt
freshly ground pepper
1 teaspoon oregano
olive oil
3 tablespoons finely chopped parsley
1 tablespoons grated lemon rind
2 cloves garlic, finely chopped
3 tbsps butter
2 stalks celery, finely chopped
2 carrots, sliced (optional)
2 tablespoons tomato paste
1 cup dry white wine
1 (28 ounce can) diced tomatoes
1 tablespoon cornstarch
2 tablespoons cold water
6 slices lemon
rice, cooked

Gremolata:
2 teaspoon grated lemon rind
2 cloves garlic, minced
1½ tablespoons finely chopped parsley

Put oven rack in middle position and preheat to 350°. Bring demi-glace to a simmer in a 1 quart saucepan over moderate heat. Remove from heat and keep warm, partially covered. Pat shanks dry and sprinkle with sa nd pepper. Dredge shanks in flour to coat, shaking off excess. Heat oil 1 a 5 to 6 quart wide heavy ovenproof pot over moderately high heat ntil just smoking, then brown shanks on all sides, about 10 minutes total, nd transfer with tongs to a plate. Add butter to pot and heat until foam ubsides, then sauté onions, carrots, celery, and garlic, stirring occasionally, ntil onions are softened, about 9 minutes. Add wine, scraping up any rown bits, then add warm demi-glace, tomatoes, and bay leaf. Return hanks (with any juices accumulated on plate) to pot and bring liquid to boil, then cover pot and braise shanks in oven until meat is very tender, bout 2 ½ hours. Carefully transfer shanks with a slotted spoon to a clean late and keep warm, loosely covered with foil. Skim fat from sauce, then immer, uncovered, on top of stove, stirring occasionally, until slightly rickened, about 15 minutes. Season sauce with salt and pepper and add hanks, then cook over low heat until heated through. (Discard strings and ay leaf before serving.) Combine the cornstarch with water and stir into ot juices. Return to the oven uncovered, and continue cooking 10 minutes ntil the juices have thickened. Garnish with lemon slices and gremolata nd serve over rice. Serves 6.

Veal Cordon Bleu

8 veal scallops (pounded 1/8 inch thick)
4 slices prosciutto
4 slices provolone cheese
Kitchen Bouquet
salt
freshly ground black pepper
flour
oil for frying

Pound veal very thin. Put slice of prosciutto and cheese on veal or chicken. Top with another slice of veal or chicken, again pounding to flatten. Brush with Kitchen Bouquet, then sprinkle with salt and freshly ground black pepper. Dust lightly with flour. Heat oil in small pan and brown them on or two at a time. Place on warm platter until serving time. Serves 4.

Veal Piccata

3 lbs veal scallops, 2 x 3 inches, pound thin
2 teaspoon salt
⅓ cup butter
freshly ground black pepper
½ cup chicken broth
1 lemon, sliced
⅓ cup fresh lemon juice
½ cup chopped parsley

Sprinkle veal with salt and freshly ground black pepper. Sauté over medium heat for 2 minutes per side or until they are brown and tender, turning once. Do as many pieces as fit your skillet; use butter as needed. Pour off fat from skillet and add chicken broth, stirring to deglaze pan, then put all the pieces back into pan. Before serving, add lemon juice and parsley. Cook over medium heat, stirring until hot. Transfer to a platter. Serve with lemon.

Note: Good served with spinach noodles and fresh tomato sauce.

My Veal Parmigiano

8 veal cutlets
¼ cup grated Parmesan
2 eggs, beaten
½ teaspoon salt
⅛ teaspoon pepper
1 cup fine dry bread crumbs
6 tablespoons olive oil
2 cups freshly made Tomato Sauce (*see recipe page 281)
8 ounces fresh mozzarella cheese

Combine Parmesan, eggs, salt and pepper and beat well. Dip cutlets i
egg in mixture; dredge in breadcrumbs. Sauté cutlets in oil in a skille
medium, heat 4 minutes on each side or until browned. Place cutlets i
a well-greased 2-quart casserole. Pour fresh tomato sauce over veal; to
with mozzarella. Bake at 350° for 15 minutes or until cheese melts. Yiel
4 servings

Grilled Lamb Chops

amb chops - 1 inch thick
emon juice
ry mustard
Herbes de Provence
alt
arlic salt
int jelly

ub chops with all ingredients. Barbecue over gray coals (4 to 8 minutes
er side) do not overcook. Serve immediately.

ote: Serve with walnut-romaine salad, mint jelly or sauce, fresh tomatoes
nd Montrachet in summer, or baked tomatoes stuffed with Spinach
Madeleine (*see recipe page 238) in winter.

Marinated Lamb Chops

8 lamb rib chops
1 whole lemon, ground
lemon juice
3 tablespoons olive oil, divided
¼ cup parsley, minced
¾ teaspoon salt
1 teaspoon tarragon leaves
1 clove garlic, minced

Trim fat from chops. Combine ground lemon with enough lemon juice to
make 1/3 cup. In a small bowl, combine lemon and juice, 2 tablespoons
olive oil, parsley, salt, tarragon and garlic. Pour marinade over chops
seal tightly, and marinate for at least 1 hour, or overnight. Shake or turn
occasionally. Drain chops. Dry with paper towels. Pan-fry chops using
remaining 1 tablespoon oil about 3 to 4 minutes each side or until done
Return reserved marinade to skillet and deglaze, reducing sauce by half
Add 2 tablespoons lemon juice to marinade. Put chops on heated platter
Either pour sauce over chops or serve on side. Note: Good served with
tomatoes stuffed with Spinach Madeleine (*see recipe page 238) and
buttered noodles sprinkled with poppy seed.

Lamb Cops

Coffee Roasted Lamb

1 (5 pound) leg of lamb (allow ½ pound, bone in, per person)
1 teaspoon salt
freshly ground black pepper
½ teaspoon lemon-pepper marinade
¼ cup all-purpose flour, divided
½ teaspoon ground ginger
1 cup coffee

Combine salt, lemon-pepper marinade, ⅛ cup flour, and ginger. Mix well and rub over entire surface of lamb. Place on rack in a shallow roasting pan and pour coffee over lamb. Bake in a preheated 325° oven for 30 to 35 minutes per pound or until meat thermometer registers 170° for medium doneness. Baste often. When roast is done remove to a heated platter and keep warm in oven until serving.

For gravy, pour drippings into a measuring cup. Skim off and discard all but ¼ cup fat; pour drippings into skillet. Blend remaining ⅛ cup flour with a little water; stir into drippings with remaining water. Stirring constantly over medium heat about 2 minutes or until gravy boils. Add salt and pepper.

Herb-Roasted Rack of Lamb

2 racks of lamb, about 2 lbs each
2 tablespoons olive oil
1 cup plain bread crumbs
3 rosemary sprigs, lightly crushed
6 thyme sprigs, lightly crushed
2 teaspoons minced garlic
1 teaspoon paprika
salt to taste

Preheat oven to 500°. Trim the lamb of excess fat, but leave a layer of fat over the meat. Combine all remaining ingredients and rub over the meat side of the racks. Put them in a roasting pan, meaty side up, and place in the oven. Roast for 25 minutes for medium rare, or until an instant-read thermometer inserted in the center of the meat registers 135°. Remove, and let sit for five minutes. Carve the racks into chops and serve.

Note: Make sure the chine bones are removed so you can easily cut through the ribs

Leg of Lamb

1 boneless leg of lamb
6 cloves of garlic
½ cup olive oil
½ cup white vinegar
1 tablespoon balsamic vinegar
1 cup lemon juice
¼ cup fresh chopped parsley
1 teaspoon paprika
1 teaspoon curry powder
1 tablespoon freshly ground black pepper

Cut excess fat from leg of lamb. Make six deep holes into lamb and insert one pealed clove of garlic into each hole. Set aside to allow it to reach room temperature. Mix other ingredients in a bowl or baking dish large enough to accommodate the lamb. Add lamb and cover. Place in refrigerator for 6-8 hours, turning over every hour. Preheat grill. Place lamb on rotisserie skewer and put on grill. Reduce temperature to low. Cook for 2 hours brushing with remaining marinade every ½ hour. Cut into thin slices. Serves 8.

Wellshire Inn Lamb Shank

2 (4 ounce) lamb shanks
1 cup carrots, chopped
1 cup onion, chopped
1 cup celery, chopped
1 tablespoon olive oil
1 teaspoon thyme
1 teaspoon rosemary
1 teaspoon salt
freshly ground black pepper
1 cup red wine
1 cup veal stock

Heat olive oil in a sauté pan. Sauté lamb and vegetables until gold brown. Add remaining ingredients. Cover with foil and place in 350° oven and cook for about 2 hours or until very tender. Yield: 2 servings

Lamb Shanks with Mushroom Bolognese

4 lamb shanks
6 tablespoons olive oil
salt
freshly ground black pepper
¾ pound mixed fresh mushrooms such as morel, shiitake, chanterelle,
1 tablespoon minced garlic
1 cup diced onion (¼ inch dice)
½ cup diced carrot (¼ inch dice)
½ cup diced celery (¼ inch dice)
2 cups dry red wine
1 bay leaf
3 cups chicken stock or canned chicken broth
3 cups peeled, seeded, and chopped tomatoes (fresh or canned)
3 tablespoons finely chopped fresh basil
1 tablespoon finely chopped fresh oregano

Preheat the oven to 300°. Heat 3 tablespoons of the olive oil in a large, deep, ovenproof pot over medium heat until hot. Season the shanks with salt and freshly ground black pepper and brown on all sides, about 10 minutes. Remove to a plate. Raise the heat to medium-high, add the mushrooms, and do not move them until they begin to brown, about 1 minute. Season with salt and freshly ground black pepper and sauté until brown all over, about 5 minutes. Remove to another plate and reserve for final assembly. Reduce the heat to medium, add the remaining 3 tablespoons olive oil to the pot, and heat until hot. Add the garlic and sauté briefly until light brown. Add the onion, carrot, and celery, season with salt and pepper, and sauté until light brown, about 8 minutes. Add the wine and bay leaf, bring to a boil over high heat, and cook until reduced by half. Add the stock and tomatoes and bring to a boil again. Season with salt and pepper. Return the heat to the pot, cover, and place in the oven to braise until fork tender. Test at 2 hours, but the shanks may take as long as 4 hours. Let the meat cool in the liquid to room temperature. Remove shanks. Skim off the fat from the braising liquids. Pour the defatted braising liquids into a saucepan and bring to a boil over high heat. Reduce the heat and simmer for about 10 minutes, skimming the surface all the while. Add the basil and oregano. Return the shanks to the sauce and simmer gently just until heated through, then remove and keep warm. Add the mushrooms to the sauce and heat gently until warm. Serve immediately. Yield: 4 servings

Venison Tenderloin with Madeira Green Peppercorn Sauce

1 (½ pound) piece venison tenderloin, trimmed
½ teaspoon freshly ground pepper
½ teaspoon salt
1 ½ tablespoons vegetable or olive oil
¼ cup finely chopped shallots
¼ cup Madeira wine
⅓ cup beef or veal demi-glace
1 teaspoon drained green peppercorns in brine, coarsely chopped
1 teaspoon unsalted butter

Put oven rack in middle position and preheat oven to 425°. Pat venison dry and sprinkle with freshly ground black pepper and ¼ teaspoon salt. Heat oil in an ovenproof 12 inch heavy skillet over moderately high heat until just smoking, brown venison on all sides (except ends), about 3 minutes total. Transfer skillet with venison to oven and roast until thermometer inserted diagonally, 2 inches into center registers 115°, 4 to 5 minutes. Transfer venison with tongs to a plate and let stand, loosely covered with foil, 5 minutes (temperature will rise to 125° for medium-rare). While meat stands, add shallot to skillet (handle will be hot) and cook over moderate heat, stirring until golden, about 2 minutes. Add Madeira and deglaze skillet by boiling, stirring, and scraping up brown bits, until liquid is reduced by half, about 1 minute. Add demi-glace and boil, stirring, until sauce is slightly thickened, about 1 minute. Stir in peppercorns, butter, remaining ¼ teaspoon salt, and any meat juices that have accumulated on plate, then remove from heat. Cut venison into ½ inch thick slices and serve with sauce. Yield: 2 servings

Smoked Venison Hindquarter

1 venison hindquarter
1 (16 ounce) bottle Italian salad dressing
1 (12 ounce) jar currant jelly
1 cup red wine
2 tablespoons butter
½ cup currant jelly
½ lemon, juiced
½ cup water
½ cup red wine
1 teaspoon salt
cayenne to taste

Mix Italian dressing, jar of currant jelly and cup of red wine. Place hindquarter of venison in heavy plastic bag with marinade and marinade in refrigerator 2 or 3 days. Remove from marinade and cook on grill until thermometer reaches 160° (4 to 7 hours). Put the reserved marinade in the pan under the roast while smoking. If preferred (or bad weather), can be cooked in oven at 325°, 30 minutes per pound, basting with the reserved marinade. To prepare hot wine sauce: melt 2 tbsp butter, add ½ cup currant jelly, lemon juice, wine, water, 1 tsp salt and cayenne. Mix with pan drippings and whisk into smooth gravy. Remove from heat and add ½ cup red wine. If venison is cooked on a grill, you can save and cook a little venison separately for drippings!

Kitchen Surgery

My operating arena has changed
Mrs. Poulet lies on my cutting board
Fully anesthetized from decapitation
She had an overnight pre-op in brine solution

Ungloved I grab my scalpel.
Shall I amputate, debride or disjoint her?
With meticulous incisions I will transform her
She will become a delectable entrée.

Vegetables & Side Dishes

Asparagus Loaf au Gratin

1 (16 ounce) can asparagus tips, reserving liquid
pimento strips (2-3 ounce jar)
2 tablespoons butter
4 tablespoons flour
1 cup milk
¼ cup liquid from asparagus
½ teaspoon salt
⅛ teaspoon freshly ground pepper
2 cups grated cheese
1 ¾ cups fine soft bread crumbs
2 eggs, slightly beaten

Preheat oven to 325°. Grease loaf pan and alternate asparagus and pimento strips across bottom. Melt butter in a saucepan, whisk in flour, cooking for one minute, slowly whisk in milk and asparagus liquid. Cook until thickened. Add salt, pepper and cheese, stir until cheese melts. Stir in crumbs, beaten eggs and fold in remaining asparagus tips, which have been cut into small pieces. Pour into loaf pan. Place the filled loaf pan in another pan of hot water. Bake in oven for 1 hour or until firm. You may need to double sauce, depending on size of the loaf pan.

Asparagus Soufflé

3 tablespoons butter
3 tablespoons flour
1 cup milk
3 eggs, separated
salt
pepper
dash ground nutmeg
¼ teaspoon whole basil leaves
1 cup finely chopped asparagus
3 tablespoons grated parmesan

Melt butter in heavy saucepan, blend in flour and cook 1 minute stirring constantly. Gradually add milk; cook over medium heat, stirring constantly until thickened. Beat egg yolks; add a small amount of white sauce to the yolks and mix. Stir yolk mixture into the remaining white sauce. Stir in seasonings, asparagus, and cheese. Beat egg whites until stiff, fold into asparagus mixture. Spoon into a greased 1 ½ quart soufflé or casserole dish. Bake at 375° about minutes. Serve immediately.

Fresh Asparagus with Sauce

30 small fresh asparagus spears
1 ½ cups water, divided
1 teaspoon salt, divided
1 clove garlic, cut in half
3 tablespoons butter, melted
1 tablespoon lemon juice
freshly ground pepper
paprika

Wash the asparagus; snap the tender tops off the asparagus spears (use about the top 4 inches of the spear). Set aside the bottom of the spears. In a saucepan, add ¾ cup water and ½ teaspoon salt. Stand the asparagus upright to keep only the bottoms in the water. Cover the pan, and bring water to a hard boil. Reduce heat to a gentle boil, and cook for 10 minutes or just until tender. While the tops are cooking, select ½ of the largest asparagus bottoms that were set aside. Using a vegetable peeler, remove the outside layer of stalk, and cut the remaining inside stalk into 1 inch pieces. In a saucepan, add remaining ¾ cup water, ½ teaspoon salt, garlic clove, and asparagus pieces. Cover, bring to a hard boil; reduce heat and cook about 8 minutes or until tender (do not allow the water to evaporate). Drain the cooked pieces, and puree in blender or processor along with the cooked garlic. Add the margarine and lemon juice and puree again. Drain the hot asparagus spears; place gently on a warm plate and spoon the pureed sauce over the spears. Sprinkle with freshly ground black pepper and paprika.

Italian Stuffed Artichokes

6 artichokes
6 cups bread crumbs
1 pound American cheese, cubed
2 bunches green onions, chopped
½ cup chopped parsley
1 cup olives, chopped
1 teaspoon garlic powder
1 teaspoon oregano
1/4 teaspoon cayenne pepper
 salt and pepper to taste
1 ½ cups olive oil
2 cup grated Romano cheese
6 thin slices lemon

Wash artichokes thoroughly after cutting about ½ off the top (the object is to remove points from ends of leaves). Reserve until ready to use. Mix all ingredients except oil, Romano cheese, and lemon slices. After thoroughly mixing, pack tightly in a pan. Gradually pour olive oil over stuffing until oil can no longer be absorbed. Open artichokes from center. Stuff every green leaf, packing tightly. Place a thin slice of lemon on top of each artichoke and sprinkle with Romano cheese. Wrap in foil. Steam until tender-approximately 1 ½ hours.
Yield: serves 6

Stuffed Pickled Beets

1 16 ounce jar pickled beets, whole
½ cup yogurt
1 cup cottage cheese
1 teaspoon chopped chives
salt and white pepper

Scoop out centers of beets with melon baller. Mix yogurt and cottage cheese, add salt and pepper to taste. Stuff with mixture of yogurt, cottage cheese and chives. Serves 8.

Flemish Red Cabbage

tablespoons olive oil

tart apples, cored and coarsely chopped

tablespoons butter

head purple cabbage, cored and shredded

tablespoons sugar (or to taste)

alt and pepper to taste

tablespoon juniper berries

tablespoon vinegar

Heat olive oil in Dutch oven. Add cabbage, sprinkle with vinegar, dot with butter, and juniper berries; season with salt and pepper. Cover and cook about 40 minutes. Add apples and sugar to taste, continue cooking until apples get tender. Correct seasonings, then serve. Serves 6-8.

Eugene Walter's Green Bean Soufflé

1 pound green beans
4 tablespoons butter
1 tablespoons flour
2 cups milk, scalded
salt and freshly ground pepper
4 tablespoons grated parmesan cheese
2 egg whites, beaten stiff
2 egg yolks

Cook beans in boiling salted water until just tender. Put 2 tablespoon
butter in a saucepan and melt over medium heat. Stir in flour cooking unti
smooth, gradually add milk until thickened and smooth, about 10 minute:
Season to taste. Remove from heat and beat in egg yolks. Place remainin
butter in skillet and sauté beans about 3 minutes. Puree beans and add t
sauce. Beat egg whites until stiff and fold into mixture along with grate
cheese. Pour into well buttered soufflé dish and bake at 350° for 30- 3.
minutes.

Fresh Green Beans and New Potatoes

2 pounds fresh green beans, trimmed and cut
1 tablespoon Goya ham seasoning
12 small Baldwin County new potatoes
2 teaspoons salt

Add ham seasoning and salt to enough water to cover beans in a deep saucepan. With vegetable peeler, peel a strip circumferentially from the mid portion of each potato. Set potatoes aside. Bring beans to a boil and lower heat to medium and cook beans about thirty minutes before adding potatoes. Add potatoes and cook until potatoes are tender when pierced with a fork. Note: *I use ham seasoning, such as a package of Goya, instead of bacon drippings or ham hock when cooking green vegetables, such as green beans or turnip greens. You do not sacrifice taste, yet end with a heart-healthy and low-cal dish.

Green Bean and Water Chestnut Casserole

1 can green beans, drained
1 can water chestnuts, drained
1 can mushroom soup
1 diced pimiento
1 can French fried onion rings

Mix beans, sliced water chestnuts, mushroom soup and pimiento. Top with rings. Bake for 15 to 20 minutes at 350º.

Good vegetable to accompany chicken livers and fruit salad. Yield: 4 servings

Better Baked Beans

2 (40-ounce) cans of pork and beans (Heinz or Bush)
2 large chopped onions
1 large chopped green pepper
1 tablespoons mustard
2 tablespoons Worcestershire
½ cup dark molasses
6 strips bacon
½ cup brown sugar

Combine beans, onions, pepper, mustard and Worcestershire and molasses. Chop fine two pieces of the bacon and stir into beans. Top casserole with the remaining strips of bacon. Bake at 275° for 3 to 4 hours. Yield: 16 servings
Note: The secret to the recipe is the long, slow cooking.
Source: My Fare Ladle (Beeland family cookbook)

Puree of Green Peas with Capers

3 pounds fresh green peas or 2 packages frozen
½ cup boiling water
salt
freshly ground pepper
⅛ teaspoon brown sugar
¼ stick butter
1 tablespoon drained capers
pimento (optional)

Cook peas covered in ½ cup boiling water with a sprinkling of salt, freshly ground black pepper and ⅛ teaspoon of brown sugar for 8 to 10 minutes. Drain, reserving liquid. Process, add butter. Reheat before serving, add liquid as necessary. Add drained, rinsed, dry capers. Decorate top with pimiento, if desired. Yield: 8 servings

Green Peas with Bacon and Mushrooms

3 slices bacon
5 tablespoons flour
¼ cup chopped onion
salt
1 cup half and half
freshly ground black pepper
2 cups sliced mushrooms
1 ½ lbs fresh tiny green peas

Fry the bacon until crisp, then drain and reserve drippings. Add the flour to the bacon drippings and make roux. Cook roux over medium heat until it begins to turn to a caramel brown color. Add the onion and cook 3 minutes. Whisk in the half and half until smooth. Gently fold in the mushrooms and peas. Heat thoroughly and pour into serving dish. Crumble the bacon on top and serve immediately. Yield: 8 servings

Maple Acorn Squash

4 medium acorn squash
1 teaspoon cinnamon
¼ teaspoon cloves
¼ cup butter
¾ cup maple syrup
½ teaspoon nutmeg
½ teaspoon salt
2 slices bacon, quartered

Cut each squash in half; remove seeds and fibers. Arrange the halves, cut side up in a large shallow baking pan. In a small bowl, blend together the syrup, cinnamon, nutmeg, cloves, salt, and butter. Spoon about 2 tablespoons of the mixture into the hollow of each squash. Top with a piece of bacon. Add boiling water to pan, about 1 inch deep. Bake in a preheated 350° oven until tender, about 1 hour. Yield: 8 servings

Squash Stuffed with Green Peas

5 yellow squash
¼ pound fresh mushrooms
1 ½ cups green peas
1 cup chicken broth
2 tablespoons lemon juice
1 ¼ teaspoons salt, divided
¼ cup dry white wine
pinch mace

Slice mushrooms and place in small boiler in water to cover. Add lemon juice to acidulate the water when cooking mushrooms. Cook on medium heat until tender. Cook whole squash in salted water (1 teaspoon salt added) for 7 minutes, or until just tender. Do not overcook or the squash shells will not hold their shape. When squash are cool enough to handle, slice off top and scoop pulp out, leaving about a ¼ inch shell. Save squash pulp for other uses. Cook green peas in chicken broth until tender. Add cooked mushrooms with their liquid, a pinch of mace, and white wine. Continue to cook until liquid reduces by half. Fill squash with peas and mushrooms. May be prepared and reheated in microwave or 350° oven about 20 to 30 minutes or until warm.

Happy New Year Peas

1 pound dried black-eyed peas (soak overnight)
3 cups water or enough to cover peas
1 pound link sausage
1 small onion, chopped
1 tablespoon prepared mustard
3 tablespoons brown sugar
1 teaspoon salt
8 ounces prepared barbecue sauce

Cook peas in water until just tender. Drain and retain ½ the liquid. Brown sausage and onion together. Drain. Place peas in a 3 qt casserole. Add sausage and onions. Stir in liquid, brown sugar, mustard, salt and barbecue sauce. Bake for 1½ in a 200º oven. Serve over rice with garlic bread.

Baby Carrots in Ginger Marmalade Glaze

1 pound baby carrots, peeled and trimmed
1 tablespoons butter
3 tablespoons ginger marmalade

Bring 6 cups water to a boil. Add carrots and boil until tender crisp. Drain and refresh in cold water. Melt butter and marmalade in a large skillet. Add carrots and shake pan to coat. Cook on low until carrots are heated.

Carrot and Broccoli Rabe Terrine

6 tablespoons unsalted butter, plus more for coating
1 pound carrots, sliced crosswise ¼ inch thick
½ cup water
salt
freshly ground pepper
6 ounces broccoli rabe—thick stems discarded; the rest chopped
5 large eggs
4 ounce shiitake mushrooms, stemmed, caps thinly sliced
4 ounces sharp white cheddar cheese, shredded

Preheat the oven to 400°. In a large, deep skillet, melt 4 tablespoons of the butter. Add the carrots and water. Cover and cook over moderately low heat, stirring occasionally, until the carrots are tender, about 30 minutes. Uncover, raise the heat to high and boil off any excess water. Season with salt and freshly ground pepper. Meanwhile, in a large skillet, melt 1 tablespoon of the butter. Add the broccoli rabe, cover and cook over moderately high heat until just tender, about 2 minutes. Season with salt and freshly ground black pepper and transfer to a bowl. Lightly beat 1 of the eggs and stir into the broccoli rabe. Wipe out the skillet and melt the remaining 1 tablespoon of butter. Add the shiitake, season with salt and freshly ground black pepper and cook over moderately high heat, stirring until tender, about 5 minutes. Line an 8 ½ x 4 ½ inch metal loaf pan with foil. Butter the foil. In a large bowl, using a pastry cutter or 2 sharp knives, coarsely chop the carrots. Lightly beat the remaining 4 eggs and add them to the carrots with the shiitake, cheddar, 1 ½ teaspoons of salt and ½ teaspoon of freshly ground black pepper. Spread half of the carrot mixture in the prepared loaf pan in an even layer. Top with the broccoli rabe mixture. Cover with the remaining carrot mixture, smoothing the surface. Set the loaf pan in a large baking dish. Add enough hot water to the dish to reach halfway up the side of the loaf pan. Bake for about 1 hour and 15 minutes, or until the cake is firm throughout. Let cool for 10 to 15 minutes. Unmold the carrot terrine onto a platter. Cut into 1 inch thick slices and serve. The baked carrot terrine can be refrigerated overnight in the pan. Bring to room temperature, cover with foil, and reheat in a hot water bath in a 350° oven until heated through, about 30 minutes.

Serves: 6

Elmira's Corn

6 ears fresh corn
2 tablespoons bacon drippings
2 tablespoons flour
water
salt to taste
freshly ground pepper

Cut kernel tops off corn, then scrape (don't cut close to cob, scrape only)
Put corn, flour, salt and freshly ground black pepper in bowl and mix. Put
½ inch water in iron skillet, bring to a boil and add corn mixture. Decrease
heat and cook slowly, stirring often and adding enough water to prevent
sticking and to maintain desired consistency. Add 2 tablespoons bacon
drippings. Note: I substitute a ham bouillon cube for the bacon drippings
to reduce fat!!

Burgundy Mushrooms

pound mushrooms, trimmed and cleaned
water
tablespoons lemon juice
tablespoons butter
cup burgundy
½ tablespoons marmite or beef extract
alt to taste
ornstarch (optional)

Bring a quart of water and lemon juice to a boil. Add mushrooms and return
to a boil. Cook 2 minutes and drain. Melt butter and sauté mushrooms until
liquid evaporated and mushrooms begin to brown. Remove mushrooms
with a slotted spoon. Deglaze pan with burgundy, add beef extract and salt
(sparingly) to taste. Return mushrooms to pan and keep warm. If thickened
sauce is preferred, mix a little cornstarch (about ½ tablespoon) with enough
water to make a paste and add to the sauce. Yield: 4 servings

Grilled Corn on the Cob with Jalapeno-Lime Butter

2 jalapeño chiles
½ cup (1 stick) butter, room temperature
1 garlic clove, minced
1 teaspoon grated lime peel
6 ears fresh corn, unhusked

To make the jalapeño-lime butter, use a broiler or gas burner to char the chiles. Grill chiles until charred on all sides. Cool 5 minutes. Using small paring knife, peel chiles. Scrape out seeds and pale membranes; discard. Coarsely chop chiles; transfer to processor. Add butter, garlic, and lime peel; process until smooth. Season the jalapeño-lime butter to taste with salt. Transfer to small bowl. Can be made 1 day ahead. Cover and chill. Bring to room temperature before serving. Grill corn until husks are black on all sides, turning occasionally, about 15 minutes. Wearing oven mitts to protect hands, remove husks and silk from corn. Serve immediately with jalapeño-lime butter and salt. Yield: 6 servings

Spinach, Broccoli and Boursin Timbale

½ cup chicken or turkey broth

1 cup heavy cream

1 cup broccoli, cooked and well chopped

½ cup spinach, cooked, squeezed dry and well chopped

2 ounces Boursin cheese

5 eggs

½ teaspoon dry mustard

½ teaspoon Worcestershire

dash Tabasco

4 tablespoons grated Parmesan

3 tablespoons chopped chives

1 tablespoon unsalted butter, room temperature

8 whole spinach leaves, steamed

Preheat oven to 350°. Combine broth and cream; reserve. Place broccoli, spinach, Boursin, and 4 tablespoons of broth and cream mixture in food processor fitted with steel blade. Process until smooth and reserve. In a separate bowl, combine eggs, mustard, Worcestershire, Tabasco, and remaining broth cream mixture, whisking well. Fold in broccoli-spinach mixture. Add Parmesan and chives. Blend thoroughly. Butter 8 timbale molds (4 ounce molds). Drape one wilted spinach leaf along bottom and sides of each mold and fill ¾ full with mixture. Place the timbales in a roasting pan high enough to be even with the ramekin. Add hot water (not boiling) to the roasting pan ¾ up side of molds. Bake in 350° oven for 45 minutes. Remove timbales from water and let rest 5 minutes. To serve, invert on serving platter or individual plates. Yield: 8 servings

Spinach Madeleine

2 packages frozen chopped spinach, thawed, with liquid saved
4 tablespoons butter
2 tablespoons flour
½ cup evaporated milk
½ cup reserved spinach juice
2 tablespoons onion, chopped
freshly ground pepper
¾ teaspoon celery salt
¾ teaspoon garlic salt
1 tbsp Worcestershire
dash red pepper
1 jalapeño pepper

Melt butter, stir in flour and cook 1-2 minutes, then add the milk and spinach juice. Cook until slightly thick. Add remaining ingredients, adding spinach last. Pour into 1 1/2 quart baking dish or individual ramekins. Bake 1 hour at 350 °. Yield: 6 servings

Note: I like to stuff tomatoes with Spinach Madeleine. Cut top off of tomato, scoop it out, salt shells and drain upside down for about thirty minutes. Before serving, stuff the shells, sprinkle bread crumbs on top and bake 30 minutes in a 325° oven.

Edna Mae's Okra and Tomatoes

5 large tomatoes, cored and chopped
1 tablespoon butter
½ teaspoon salt
2 cups okra, cut into rounds
¼ teaspoon freshly ground black pepper

Put tomatoes, butter, salt and freshly ground black pepper in large covered pot. Stew for 4 to 6 hours (the longer the better); 15 to 30 minutes before ready to serve, add okra and continue to stew until okra is tender.
Note: To make succotash, add corn or lima beans to stewed tomatoes and/ or okra!

Scalloped Tomatoes & Artichokes

1 large can tomatoes, drained
1 can artichoke hearts, drained
⅓ cup chopped onion
2 tablespoons chopped scallions
¼ pound butter
1 tablespoons basil
2 teaspoons sugar
¾ teaspoon salt
¼ teaspoon freshly ground black pepper

Preheat oven to 325°. Sauté onions. Add other ingredients. Bake for 3 minutes. Yield: 4 servings

Rosemary Stuffed New Potato

8 Baldwin County new potatoes
olive oil
salt
freshly ground black pepper
fresh rosemary

Preheat oven to 450°. Parboil whole new potatoes until just barely tender, yet still very firm. Roll the warm potatoes in olive oil. Sprinkle with salt and freshly ground black pepper. Make three to four slices about ¾ way into potato being careful to not cut through and to keep the potato intact. Strip rosemary from stem and stuff rosemary into the slices. Roast stuffed potatoes for about twenty or 30 minutes.

Rosemary Stuffed New Potato

Pommes Anna (Potatoes Anna)

1 teaspoon kosher or sea salt
½ teaspoon freshly ground pepper
2 ½ tablespoons unsalted butter
3 pounds peeled baking potatoes, cut into
⅛ inch slices
1 tablespoon unsalted butter, melted
1 tablespoon fresh flat-leaf parsley (optional)

Preheat oven to 450°. Combine salt and freshly ground black pepper in a small bowl. Melt 2 ½ tablespoons butter in a 10 inch cast-iron or ovenproof heavy skillet over medium heat. Arrange a single layer of potato slices slightly overlapping, in a circular pattern in pan; sprinkle with ¼ teaspoon salt and freshly ground black pepper mixture. Drizzle ½ teaspoon melted butter over potatoes. Repeat the layers 5 times, ending with butter. Press firmly to pack. Cook over medium-low heat until 30 minutes. Using bottom of 9 inch cake pan, press potatoes down firmly to compact. Cover skillet and place in oven. Bake until potatoes begin to soften, about 20 minutes. Uncover and continue to bake until potatoes are tender when paring knife is inserted in center and edge of potatoes near skillet is browned, about 10 minutes longer. Meanwhile, line rimless cookie sheet or back of a baking sheet with foil and coat very lightly with oil. Drain off excess fat from potatoes by pressing potatoes into skillet with bottom of cake pan while tilting skillet to pour off fat. Set foil lined cookie sheet on top of skillet. With hands protected by oven mitts or potholders, hold cookie sheet in place with one hand and carefully invert skillet and cookie sheet together. Remove skillet. Carefully slide potatoes onto platter; cut into wedges and serve immediately. Serves 8

Scalloped Potatoes

2 quarts potatoes, sliced thin
1/2 cup green bell pepper, chopped
1/2 cup chopped onion
1/2 teaspoon garlic salt
1/2 cup parmesan or Swiss cheese (can use larger amount)
2 teaspoons salt
1/4 teaspoon freshly ground black pepper
1/2 cup ripe olives, chopped (optional)
1 (10 ounce) can cream of mushroom soup
1 cup milk or 1/2 and 1/2
1/2 cup butter

Alternate layers of potato, green pepper, and onion in a greased baking dish. Sprinkle with all the seasonings and olives (if used). In a saucepan, heat together the soup, milk, and butter. Pour over all and bake covered at 350° for 45 minutes. Uncover, bake 30 minutes more. Sour cream can be substituted for milk. May top with Swiss cheese combined with bread crumbs. Omit Parmesan when using Swiss cheese.

Roasted Potatoes Provencale

1 pound red potatoes, cut into ½ inch dice
2 cloves garlic, chopped
2 tablespoons olive oil
salt to taste
10 Kalamata or brine-cured olives, pitted and chopped
1 ½ tablespoons minced fresh parsley leaves
salt and freshly ground pepper to taste

Preheat oven to 425°. In a baking pan, toss well the potatoes and garlic in the oil. Roast the mixture, stirring occasionally, for 25 minute or until it is golden. Transfer the mixture to a serving dish and stir in olives and parsley. Sprinkle with salt and freshly ground black pepper to taste. Serves 2

Rosemary Skewered Roasted New Potatoes

16 small Baldwin County new potatoes
olive oil
salt
freshly ground black pepper
4 rosemary sprigs

Preheat oven to 450°. Parboil new potatoes. Put potatoes in olive oil and roll to cover. Lightly salt and pepper potatoes. Thread 4 small potatoes onto twig of rosemary (strip leaves away to within and inch of top of sprig, before threading). Roast skewered potatoes until lightly browned (about 30 minutes). Cherry tomatoes can be interspersed with potatoes before roasting.

Pureed Sweet Potatoes

5 medium sweet potatoes, all about the same size
⅔ stick butter
¼ cup half and half, warmed
¼ cup orange juice
zest from two oranges
pinch ground ginger
1 teaspoon cinnamon
Pinch nutmeg
1 tablespoon Bourbon whiskey
3 tablespoons cane syrup
⅛ teaspoon salt

Prick the sweet potatoes about six times with a kitchen fork. Place the sweet potatoes on the turntable of the microwave oven like the spokes of a wheel, atop a layer of paper towels. Microwave on high for seven minutes, then turn them over (careful - they may be very hot). Microwave another seven minutes. Let them stand in the microwave for about seven more minutes, then check to see if they're soft. If not, microwave in two-minute bursts until the potatoes are fully soft. As soon as the potatoes have cooled enough to safely handle, scoop them into the food mill and crank them through into a bowl. If you do not have a food mill, mash the potatoes with the tines of a fork (do not use a processor). Add the butter and the cream, and whisk until blended. Add all the other ingredients, and whisk until smooth. If you want to add an extra touch, you can load the sweet potatoes into a shallow glass baking dish, sprinkle a little brown sugar over the top, and bake it again until a crust forms. Serves eight
Source: Tom Fitzmorris

Sweet Potato Soufflé

1 cup milk
½ cup sugar
½ teaspoon salt
3 tablespoons butter
1 teaspoon nutmeg
2 cup sweet potatoes, mashed
2 eggs, separated
½ cup raisins
½ cup chopped pecans
4-6 marshmallows

Scald milk and add sugar, salt, butter, nutmeg and potatoes; beat until fluffy (do not use processor). Beat egg yolks and add to potatoes. Add raisins and pecans. Beat egg whites stiff, fold into potatoes and pour into greased baking dish. Bake in moderate oven (350°.) 50 to 60 minutes or until firm. Top with sliced marshmallows and brown in oven. Yield: 8 servings

Sweet Potato Soufflé In Orange Cups

1 cup milk
½ cup sugar
½ teaspoon salt
3 tablespoons butter
1 teaspoon nutmeg
2 cup sweet potatoes, mashed
2 eggs, separated
½ cup raisins
½ cup chopped pecans
4 marshmallows, sliced into slices (use knife dipped in water to slice
    marshmallows)
4 oranges, halved and pulp removed to make cups

Scald milk and add sugar, salt, butter, nutmeg and potatoes; beat until fluffy (do not use processor). Beat egg yolks and add to potatoes. Add raisins and pecans. Beat egg whites until stiff, fold into potatoes. Stuff the orange cups with the mixture. Bake in moderate oven (350*.) 30 to 40 minutes. Top with sliced marshmallows and toast in oven (under broiler, watching carefully so they do not burn).

Note: This is an OLD family favorite recipe served Thanksgiving and Christmas along with the traditional turkey. The removed orange sections were reserved to make Ambrosia (*see recipe page 339)

Candied Yams

6 medium sweet potatoes (about 4 ½ pounds)
⅓ cup firmly packed brown sugar
10 tablespoons sugar
¼ teaspoon nutmeg
¼ teaspoon allspice
1 teaspoon cinnamon
2 tablespoons flour
¾ cup pineapple juice
½ cup light corn syrup
2 tablespoons orange juice
¼ cup butter
½ cup chopped pecans

Cook sweet potatoes in boiling water 20 to 25 minutes or until fork tender. Let cool to touch; peel and cut potatoes lengthwise into ¼ inch slices. Set aside. Combine brown sugar and next 5 ingredients in saucepan; stir in pineapple juice, syrup, orange juice, and butter. Cook over medium heat about 10 minutes, stirring occasionally. Place half of sweet potatoes in a lightly greased 13 x 9 x 2 inch baking dish. Pour half of sugar mixture over potatoes; repeat layers. Sprinkle with pecans. Bake at 350° for 30 minutes or until bubbly. Yield: 8 servings

Moonlight, Basil and Spinakopita

What a beautiful and magic night..
My heart is filled with totally unexpected joy, pleasure and happiness
A special friend had shared a recipe which I had postponed trying….
Tonight I entered the kitchen with no expectations except spinakopita….

With no dinner entrée in mind, only a vine ripened tomato beckoned
I thought of the basil in mon potager, now threatened by the season
Ventured out my kitchen door with an unneeded light in hand
A full harvest moon greeted me and my moon talisman

My large oak had opened its branches so the moon could shine through
My basil stood there verdant and bolting in the moonlight
Knowing that its days were numbered, I liberally snipped above the nodes
While admiring the plants' erections and strengths in their last days

Back to the kitchen and my eagerly anticipated first attempt at spinakopita
Having been shown phyllo's great resiliency, no longer did I fear phyllo
Moonbeams followed me inside and I proceeded with great joy in my heart
Loving moon shadows by my side…

Fruits

Heavenly Cranberry Sauce

2 pounds fresh cranberries
2 cups walnuts, coarsely chopped
3 cups sugar
2 lemons, grated whole after de-seeding
2 cups orange marmalade

Wash and drain cranberries. Put in shallow 2 quart baking dish. Top with layer of nuts, next sugar, then juice and grated rind of lemons, and next the marmalade. Cover tightly with foil and bake for 45 minutes at 350°.

Cranberry And Orange Salad Mold

3 ounce package black cherry Jello
cup hot water
tbsp gelatin
¼ cup sugar
2 tbsps lemon juice
cup pineapple juice
cup crushed pineapple, drained
2 cups raw cranberries, ground
2 whole oranges
cup chopped pecans

Dissolve cherry gelatin in hot water. Add sugar and lemon juice. Soak in pineapple juice and dissolve over hot water. Add to cherry gelatin. When gelatin begins to thicken, add other ingredients and pour into mold.

Apple Cheese Casserole

1 stick butter
1 cup brown sugar
8 ounces sharp cheddar, grated
¾ cup flour
1 can (20 ounce) sliced Lucky Leaf apples

Cream butter and sugar in bowl. Add cheese, continue beating until blended. Add flour and mix well. Put apples in buttered casserole with cheese mixture. Bake in 350° oven 30-45 minutes. Serves 6-8.

Baked Stuffed Apples

8 cooking apples (preferably gala), cored
1 ½ cups dry red wine
4 tablespoons brown sugar
4 teaspoon honey
½ cup currants
1 teaspoon grated orange zest
1 teaspoon cinnamon
1 ½ tablespoons butter
crème fraîche
½ cup chopped pecans or walnuts

Soak currants in the wine for 30 minutes. Drain, reserve wine. Stuff the apples with pecans or walnuts, currants, and zest. Put ½ tsp brown sugar and ½ tsp honey atop stuffing. Place apples upright in a buttered baking dish and dot each with butter. Pour reserved wine over the apples. Bake in a preheated 400° oven for 30-40 minutes or until tender, basting every 10 minutes. Serve hot or cold with crème fraîche. Yield: 8 servings

Pear Halves filled with Mint

4 pear halves (fresh or canned)
mint jelly

Fill pear halves with mint jelly and bake in moderate oven until jelly melts
and pears are heated through. If using fresh pears, you will need to heat
them for 30-40 minutes. Yield: 4 servings
Note: Good accompaniment for lamb dishes!

Pears Baked With Blue Cheese And Port

4 Bosc or Bartlett pears peeled, halved and cored
½ cup port wine
½ cup honey
4 tablespoons bleu cheese

Preheat oven to 350°. Bake pears with port and honey, uncovered basting with pan juices, 30 minutes or until tender. Place a generous tablespoon cheese in center of each pear half. Heat in oven 1 minute or until cheese is partially melted.

Honey Roasted Kumquats - Cranberry Stuffed

24 kumquats
honey
Heavenly Cranberries

Preheat oven to 450°. Put kumquats in pan with warm water. Bring to a boil and boil 5 minute until softened. While warm, roll in honey and place on foil lined tray for about 15 minutes in 450° oven. When cool enough to handle, squeeze out seeds and part of pulp. With thumb, shape the empty kumquat shell into little basket and stuff with Heavenly Cranberries

To prepare Heavenly Cranberry Sauce:
2 pounds fresh cranberries
2 cups walnuts, coarsely chopped
3 cups sugar
2 lemons, grated whole after de-seeding
2 cups orange marmalade

Wash and drain cranberries. Put in shallow 2-quart baking dish. Top with layer of nuts, next sugar, then juice and grated rind of lemons, next the marmalade. Cover tightly with foil and bake for 45 minutes at 350°.
Note: Use as garnish for turkey platter.

Honeydew Fruit Bowl

2 honeydew melons
1 cup seedless grapes
1 cup strawberries, halved
¼ cup Mandarin oranges
1 ¼ cups watermelon balls
orange rind zest
1 recipe Ginger Yogurt Dressing (*see recipe page 280)

Cut melons in half and remove seeds. Fill melon bowls with fruits, top with a dollop of dressing.

Melon Boats

1 cantaloupe
1 honeydew melon
1 wedge watermelon (optional)

Cut either melon into 2 ½ inch wedges. Cut the other melon and with
melon baller or a one teaspoon measuring spoon, scoop out melon balls
(about 5 per serving). With the melon baller remove about five balls from
each wedge. Fill the empty holes that are left with balls from the other
melon. If you have watermelon available, scoop out watermelon balls and
intersperse them with the melon when filling your wedge.
This is a refreshing addition to any breakfast menu!
Contributor: Wolfgang Wetter,
The Limestone Mansion, Cherry Valley, NY

Melon Boat

Chutney Baked Peaches

4 peach halves (canned or fresh)
chutney

Stuff fruit with chutney and bake in moderate oven until heated through. Run under broiler briefly, if desired. Yield: 4 servings Note: I like to use these as an accompaniment and garnish on the platter with a Stuffed Pork Tenderloin or Pork Roast (*see recipes)

Preserved Lemons

8-10 lemons, scrubbed very clean
½ cup kosher salt, more if needed
extra fresh squeezed lemon juice, if needed
sterilized quart canning jar

Place 2 Tbsp of salt in the bottom of a sterilized jar. One by one, prepare
the lemons in the following way. Cut off any protruding stems from the
lemons, and cut ¼ inch off the tip of each lemon. Cut the lemons as if you
were going to cut them in half lengthwise, starting from the tip, but do not
cut all the way. Keep the lemon attached at the base. Make another cut in
a similar manner, so now the lemon is quartered, but again, attached at the
base. Pry the lemons open and generously sprinkle salt all over the inside
and outsides of the lemons. Pack the lemons in the jar, squishing them
down so that juice is extracted and the lemon juice rises to the top of the
jar. Fill up the jar with lemons, make sure the top is covered with lemon
juice. Add more fresh squeezed lemon juice if necessary. Top with a couple
tablespoons of salt. Seal the jar and let sit at room temperature for a couple
days. Turn the jar upside down occasionally. Put in refrigerator and let sit
again turning upside down occasionally, for at least 3 weeks, until lemon
rinds soften. To use, remove a lemon from the jar and rinse thoroughly in
water to remove salt. Discard seeds before using. Discard the pulp before
using, if desired. Store in refrigerator for up to 6 months.

Preserved Lemmons

Curried Fruit Bake

⅔ cup brown sugar firmly packed
2 teaspoons curry powder
1 (15 ¼ ounce) can peach halves, well drained
1 (17 ounce) can dark sweet cherries, well drained
1 (20 ounce) can pineapple chunks, well drained
1 (15 ¼ ounce) can pear halves, well drained
1 (15 ounce) can mandarin oranges, well drained
2 tablespoons lemon juice
3 tablespoons butter, cut up into pieces

Combine fruit in a lightly greased 11 x 7 inch baking dish. Stir togethe
brown sugar and curry powder; sprinkle over fruit. Drizzle with lemo
juice, and dot with butter. Bake, covered, at 300° for 1 hour. Yield: 10 t
12

Spring

As a soon to be septuagenarian, I find each spring more
beautiful,stimulating and exhilarating than the ones before
What am I feeling, what does spring mean to me?
Many women see spring as "another fun shopping spree," new
clothesand exciting additions to their wardrobes
Perhaps in years past I went there; my thoughts now turn to the
kitchenand my recipe file
Loving to cook and to eat, I find the change of seasons in the kitchen so
exciting and cannot wait to go to the market and shop for
"spring dishes"
You may be thinking, "what are they?"
For some unknown reason, the grill and the outdoors always beckon
inthe spring
Being a country and farm girl, spring is synonymous with lamb
A reminder yesterday was the sudden growth spurt of mint in my little
herb garden!
In the spring I jump up each morning and run outside to see what has
awakened and sprung a leaf overnight
My plan is a smoked leg of spring lamb, fresh mint sauce and a big bowl
of the unforgettable Rocky Creek Inn cottage cheese and beet
salad of springs gone by….
Short and shrinking, I divert my thoughts from food to spring cleaning.
Having trained myself to cope with clutter, I ignore cleaning closets and
treat myself to a "box for the day" in the spring

My attic is filled with boxes labeled "keepers" that I have moved, unopened, from shore to shore, home to home, for years

Each spring I go into the attic, pick a box at random and have a wonderful time plundering through treasures and memories

Opening each box is like Christmas in the spring!

Sauces

Anchovy Dipping Sauce

2 egg yolks
4 tablespoons Dijon mustard
1 (2 ounce) can anchovies, undrained
1 lemon
1 cup vegetable oil
freshly ground black pepper
1 tablespoon capers

In a food processor, combine egg yolks, mustard, anchovies, and lemo
juice; mix until pale and foamy. With motor running, slowly add oil i
a steady stream. Add freshly ground black pepper to taste. Turn into
storage container and stir in capers. Cover and refrigerate. Yield: mak
1 ¼ cup
Note: Salty, but, delicious with crisp fresh crudités, especially ra
asparagus spears and sugar snap peas.
Contributor: Betty McGowin Miller, The Phantom Cook

Béchamel Sauce II

½ cup all purpose flour
4 tablespoons butter
½ onion, minced
4 cups milk
¼ teaspoon white pepper
¼ teaspoon nutmeg
¼ teaspoon salt
¼ pound veal, chopped

Cook flour 2-3 minutes before whisking in melted butter. Sauté onion until golden, then add it to the flour mixture. Heat milk and add, stirring continuously until it is smooth. Sauté ¼ lb veal in 2 tablespoons butter over very low heat. Season the veal with sprig of thyme or a tiny pinch of leaves. Add a pinch of white pepper and freshly grated nutmeg. Cook the veal for 5 minutes, stirring it frequently to prevent it from browning; stir it into the sauce. Cook the sauce in the top of a double boiler over hot water stirring from time to time until thickened. Strain through fine sieve and dot with bits of butter; they will melt and prevent a film from forming. Makes about quart.

For caper cream sauce:
To 1 cup of Béchamel sauce add ¼ cup capers and a teaspoon of lemon juice. Yield: 6 servings

Cheese Sauce

6 tablespoons butter
6 tablespoons flour
2 ½ cups light cream
2 teaspoons dry mustard
2 cups grated sharp cheddar cheese
1 tablespoon sherry
 salt and freshly ground black pepper

Combine flour and butter in heavy pan over heat. Cook for 2 minutes. Heat, but do not boil, cream. Gradually stir cream into flour and butter. Stir in mustard, cheese, sherry, salt, and freshly ground black pepper.

Marchand de Vin

¼ cup butter
½ cup country ham, minced
½ cup onions, minced
⅓ cup mushrooms, minced
 tablespoons garlic, minced
 tablespoons flour
Freshly ground black pepper
Salt
Cayenne
¼ cup consommé
 ½ cups red wine

Sauté ham and onions in butter, add mushrooms and garlic and continue to sauté until onions begin to take on color. Stir in flour. Season to taste. Cook for about 10 minutes or until a rich brown. Blend in consommé and red wine. Simmer, stirring often, for 35 to 40 minutes. Freezes well and also keeps well in refrigerator.

Sauce Meuniere

½ cup butter
½ teaspoon salt
1 tablespoon parsley, chopped
½ teaspoon freshly ground pepper
1 tablespoon green onions, minced
dash Tabasco
2 tablespoons lemon juice

Mix and simmer over low heat.

Macadamia Sauce For Fish

½ cup butter
½ cup macadamia nuts, chopped
1 teaspoon onion juice
1 teaspoon lemon juice
1 teaspoon finely chopped chives
salt
pepper
dash nutmeg

Melt butter in saucepan, add other ingredients and simmer gently. Pour over fish. Yield: 2 servings

Yogurt Dressing For Fresh Asparagus

1 cup plain yogurt
1 clove garlic, pressed
salt
pepper
chopped parsley or watercress
dash of Tabasco or cayenne

Mix all ingredients and chill.

Horseradish Sauce

tablespoons horseradish
Juice of one lemon
cup whipping cream

Squeeze horseradish dry in a paper towel. Combine lemon juice with horseradish. Whip cream and fold into horseradish mix. Can be made a day ahead. Contributor: James Ash

Persillade

1 bunch parsley, stems removed
6 cloves garlic

Chop together. Sprinkle over stews, soups, etc.
Note: A classic French bistro dish is Pommes Persillade, basically cubed
potatoes fried in small amount of oil, with persillade added at the end of
the cooking.

Lemon-Raisin Sauce

½ cup sugar
1 tablespoon cornstarch
1 cup water
3 tablespoons butter
½ teaspoon grated lemon rind
1 ½ tablespoons lemon juice
¼ cup raisins, plumped

Combine sugar, cornstarch, and water in top of a double boiler. Cook over water until thickened. Remove from heat. Stir in butter, rind and juice plumped (soaked in warm water and drained) raisins. Note: Good sauce for ham or gingerbread. Yield: 4-6 servings

Jezebel Sauce

1 (5 ounce) jar horseradish
1 (12 ounce) can dry mustard
1 (18 ounce) jar apple jelly
1 (18 ounce) jar pineapple preserves
2 tablespoons freshly ground pepper

Mix the horseradish and dry mustard well. Combine with remaining ingredients. Will keep in refrigerator or freezer for months. Especially good on sliced ham or with pork loin.

Yield: 4 cups

Note: While cleaning up the kitchen late one evening, I dipped a leftover cheese straw in Jezebel and discovered a new hors-d'oeuvre. Cheese straws work well if serving indoors; however, I use crisp cheese sticks for lawn or wharf.

Mock Devonshire Cream

1 package cream cheese
8 ounce sour cream
sugar to taste or 2 packages Splenda

Mix equal parts sour cream and softened cream cheese. Beat together well. Add sugar to taste. Keeps for two weeks in the refrigerator.

Ginger-Yogurt Dressing

⅔ cup plain yogurt
¼ cup chopped walnuts or almonds
1 tsp honey
1 tsp fresh ginger, diced

In a small bowl, stir together the yogurt, chopped nuts, honey, and minced ginger. Chill.

My Fresh Tomato Sauce

2 tomatoes, cored and chopped
1 handful fresh basil
½ onion, chopped
1 clove garlic, minced
2 teaspoons olive oil
salt to taste
freshly ground black pepper

Add olive oil to a skillet or saucepan with lid and heat. Add onion and garlic, turn heat to low, cover with lid and steam for 20-30 minutes. Add tomatoes, reduce heat and simmer for 5-10 minutes. Add basil and season to taste with salt and pepper. Continue to simmer over low heat for 5-10 minutes.

Old Beaux

Old beaux are like leftovers
Heat them up once
Enjoy them
Then dispose of what remains.

Grains & Cereal

BRS Jalapeño Cheese Grits

1 cup water ground grits
3 cups water
1 stick butter
1 teaspoon salt
½ roll jalapeño cheese
½ roll garlic cheese
2 eggs, separated and beaten
1 ½ tablespoons Worcestershire
½ teaspoon garlic powder
1 teaspoon Tabasco
wheat germ
paprika

Cook grits with butter in salted water until done, about 25 minutes, adding more water as necessary. Add cheeses and stir until melted and well blended. Add beaten egg yolks, Tabasco, Worcestershire, and garlic powder. Fold in stiffly beaten egg whites. Top with wheat germ and paprika. Put in a 2 quart Pyrex dish and cook at 350º until bubbly. Can be refrigerated and cooked just before serving. Freezes well (freeze before cooking and allow to thaw to room temperature before cooking and serving).
*If cheese rolls are not available, I substitute 2 jars of Old English cheese spread per roll and add minced garlic and jalapeños.

Asparagus Risotto II

½ pounds asparagus
cups (about) canned chicken broth
cup water
tablespoon butter
large onion, chopped
cups Arborio rice
½ cup dry white wine
teaspoons chopped fresh rosemary
cup freshly grated Parmesan cheese
¼ cup whipping cream
resh rosemary sprigs (optional)

Trim tough ends from asparagus; discard. Cut off asparagus tips and reserve. Cut stalks into ¾-inch-long pieces. Place ⅔ of stalk pieces, 1 cup broth, and 1 cup water in blender. Puree until smooth. Set aside. Sauté onion in butter until tender. Add rice and stir 1 minute. Add wine and cook until absorbed. Add ½ cup broth and chopped rosemary; simmer until liquid is absorbed, stirring often, about 4 minutes. Continue to cook for 15 minutes, adding more broth by ½ cupfuls and allowing liquid to be absorbed before adding more, stirring often. Add remaining asparagus stalk pieces and reserved asparagus tips and continue cooking until rice is just tender and mixture is creamy, adding broth as needed, stirring, about 10 minutes longer. Add reserved asparagus puree and stir until absorbed, about 3 minutes. Stir in ½ cup Parmesan and cream. Season to taste with salt and pepper. Transfer risotto to bowl. Garnish with rosemary sprigs, if desired. Serve with remaining Parmesan.

Peter Devin's Risotto

2 cups chicken broth
1 cup or more white wine (preferably Prosecco)
1 cup water
1 cup Arborio rice
olive oil
¼ cup prosciutto
1 head radicchio, chopped
salt
pepper
3 cloves garlic, minced
1 handful grated Parmesan

Mix wine, chicken broth, and water; keep hot in boiler. Put rice and oliv
oil in skillet, coat well and set aside. In another skillet place choppe
radicchio and prosciutto; drizzle with olive oil and sauté, add garlic an
cook a little longer, then drizzle the mixture with wine and keep on very lo
heat. Place Arborio over low heat and add hot broth mixture, a small ladl
at a time, stirring continuously. Keep adding broth in small increments an
cook until al dente. DO NOT OVERCOOK. Stir radicchio mixture into a
dente Arborio and season with salt and pepper.
*Another dry white wine can be substituted for Prosecco. Prosecco wa
the choice of the chef, who lives in Italy.
Serve immediately.

Basic Polenta

cups water

teaspoons salt

¾ cups yellow cornmeal

tablespoons unsalted butter

Bring 6 cups of water to a boil in a heavy large saucepan. Add 2 teaspoons of salt. Gradually whisk in the cornmeal. Reduce the heat to low and cook until the mixture thickens and the cornmeal is tender, stirring often, about 15 minutes. Turn off the heat. Add the butter, and stir until melted. Can spread in pan, bake, cut into wedges, etc. or fry in olive oil. Yield: 6 servings

Wild Mushroom Risotto

6 ½ cups chicken stock or 5 cups low-sodium chicken broth
1 tablespoon olive oil
½ stick unsalted butter
¼ lb fresh wild mushrooms, such as porcini, chanterelles, or hedge
⅓ cup finely chopped shallots
1 ½ cups Arborio rice
½ to 1 teaspoon white truffle oil (optional)
¾ cup finely grated Parmigiano-Reggiano
1 teaspoon chopped fresh chives

Bring stock to a simmer in a 4 quart pot and keep at a bare simmer, covered
Heat oil with 1 tablespoon butter in a 4 to 5 quart heavy saucepan over
moderately high heat until foam subsides, then sauté mushrooms, stirring
occasionally, until browned and any liquid they give off is evaporated
about 4 minutes. Season with salt and pepper, then transfer to a bowl
Cook shallots in 2 tablespoons butter in same saucepan over moderate
heat, stirring, until softened, about 3 minutes. Add rice and cook, stirring
1 minute. Ladle in 1 cup simmering stock and cook at a strong simmer
stirring, until absorbed. Continue simmering and adding stock, about ½
cup at a time, stirring very frequently and letting each addition be absorbed
before adding next, until rice is just tender and creamy-looking, 16 to 18
minutes. (Save leftover stock for thinning.) Remove from heat and stir in
remaining tablespoon butter, sautéed mushrooms, truffle oil to taste (if
using), cheese, chives, salt and pepper to taste. To thin risotto, use leftover
stock. Yield: 4 servings

Barley and Mushroom Casserole

 cup onions, chopped fine
 ½ lb fresh mushrooms
 tablespoons butter
 cup pearl barley
 ½ teaspoon salt
 ¼ teaspoon freshly ground pepper
 cups chicken broth

Sauté onions and mushrooms in butter until soft. Remove from pan. Put barley in sauté pan and brown lightly. Put barley, mushrooms, and onions in buttered casserole. Add ½ teaspoon salt, ¼ teaspoon freshly ground black pepper and 1 ½ cups broth. Cover and bake 30 minutes at 350*. Uncover, add rest of the broth and bake until barley is done. DO NOT OVERCOOK.

Pilaf from La Cuisine Classique

1 cup bulgur
2 ½ cups chicken broth
dash of allspice
dash of cinnamon
dash of cloves
dash of nutmeg
dash of cardamom seeds (removed from pod)
¼ cup currants
¼ cup pignoli (pine nuts) toasted

Carefully brown bulgur over medium heat being mindful not to burn, must stir constantly-put aside. Heat chicken broth with cardamom seed- add allspice, cinnamon, nutmeg, and cloves. Simmer. Add bulgur to broth cover and cook 5 minutes. Raise lid, toss currants in, cover pot for a few minutes.

Note: The late owner of La Cuisine Classique in New Orleans gave me this recipe (verbally) as I shopped one day in his delightful shop for treasure for my kitchen.

Bulgur Pilaf

½ cup finely chopped onion
2 tablespoons extra-virgin olive oil
1 ½ teaspoons whole coriander seeds
1 scant cup fine bulgur
1 cup boiling-hot water
⅓ cup slivered almonds, toasted
½ teaspoon salt
¼ teaspoon black pepper

Cook onion in oil in a 2 quart heavy saucepan over moderate heat, stirring occasionally, until golden brown, 5 to 7 minutes.
Meanwhile, wrap coriander seeds in a clean kitchen towel and coarsely crush by pressing with flat side of a large heavy knife.
Add coriander and bulgur to onion and cook, stirring, 2 minutes. Stir in hot water, then remove from heat and let stand, covered, until bulgur is softened, about 25 minutes. Fluff with a fork, then stir in almonds, salt, and pepper. Serve warm or at room temperature.

Wild Rice and Toasted Pecan Pilaf

1 cup pecans, chopped
2 tablespoons unsalted butter, melted
¾ teaspoon dried thyme, crumbled
¼ teaspoon salt
1 large onion, halved lengthwise and sliced thin
1 yellow bell pepper, julienned
1/4 cup olive oil
2 ½ cups wild rice (about 1 pound), rinsed well in several changes of water
4 ½ cups chicken broth

Preheat the oven to 375°. In a small baking pan toss the pecans with the butter, the thyme, and the salt until they are coated well and toast them in the middle of the oven for 10 minutes, or until they are crisp and fragrant. In a flameproof casserole cook the onion and the bell pepper in the oil over moderately low heat, stirring, for 5 minutes, or until they are just softened, and with a slotted spoon transfer them to a bowl. Add the rice to the casserole, and cook, stirring constantly, for 1 minute. Stir in the broth, pepper to taste, then bring the mixture to a boil. Bake the mixture, covered, in the middle of the oven for 40 minutes. Stir in the onion mixture, bake the pilaf, covered, for 30 minutes more, or until the rice is tender and the broth has been absorbed; stir in the pecans. Yield: serves 8

Curried Rice Pilaf

med onions, coarsely chopped
bay leaves
½ teaspoons garam masala
teaspoon curry powder
tablespoons peanut oil
cup basmati or long grain rice
tablespoons raisins
teaspoon salt
cups water
cup frozen peas
cup shredded carrots
cup toasted cashews or peanuts

large, heavy pan cook onions, bay leaves, garam masala, and curry in oil
r about 5 minutes or until onions are tender. Stir uncooked rice, raisins,
ay leaves, and salt into mixture. Carefully add water. Simmer covered
bout 10 minutes or until water is absorbed and rice tender. Stir in peas
nd shredded carrots. Cover and cook 3 to 5 minutes or more until heated.
prinkle with nuts just before serving. Yield: 6 servings

My Wild Rice Casserole

½ pound mushrooms, sliced
dash of Tabasco
dash of Worcestershire
dash lemon juice
1 cup wild rice
2 cups water
2 ½ teaspoon salt
1/2 pound chicken livers
2 tablespoons butter
¼ cup butter, melted
½ cup cream
½ cup sherry

Wash and slice mushrooms. Place in small pan with water to cover. Ad
Tabasco, Worcestershire, and lemon juice. Simmer until tender. Wash wi
rice with cold water until clear. Soak in warm water 1 hour. Then cook
double boiler with 2 cups water and salt for 1 hour. Drain. Sauté chick
livers in 2 tablespoons butter. Cool and cut into halves. Before servin
place rice in bowl and add ¼ cup melted butter, cream, sherry, mushroon
and chicken livers.

Bailey's Creek Cereal Venture

While still in an active solo Gyn practice, I was at a polo match and met young male retiree, Patrick McDonald. When introduced, he said, "I understand you like to cook." A few days later he appeared in my waiting room with a little brown bag with a note which said, "try this and I will give you a call". The package contained a delightful natural cereal unlike any that I had ever tasted. When he called, he said he was interested in marketing this product that he had created and wanted to know if I was interested. I soon learned that he was a nutrition fanatic and much more knowledgeable about food families than I.

The following year we went through the development process. We spent months importing and sampling various grains, nut and fruits, selecting packaging, designing a label, and bringing his dream to fruition. I must say that I much prefer wine tasting to grain tasting. Have you ever sat facing six samples of rolled oats and dryly tasted them, one by one, to find the superior OAT? When we finally chose an OAT and ordered, unknown to me, he had two hundred pounds of the chosen flake delivered to my medical office. The driver was baffled when he found his destination a gynecologist's office and meekly came to the desk to announce the delivery. My small waiting room suddenly became very crowded as he drug in bag after bag and deposited them amid the waiting patients.

When we finally were ready to mix, package, and market our product, the late Mrs. Pacey very kindly offered us the long marble tables at her Punta Clara Candy Kitchen to mix and package our cereal after candy hours. The cereal master insisted that we be properly attired in OR gear. He insisted that our gloves extend above the elbow. It had been decades since I had seen a V&E glove (version and extraction). When I called my medical supplier, he informed me that they had not been stocked in years. I called my favorite veterinarian, Dr. Albert Corte, and learned that they were still used in veterinarian medicine.

I would come home after a long day in surgery, enter my former sewin
room, which I had converted to a cereal packaging room, and laboriousl
weigh, package, and label the cereals. Then I would load it into my ca
and distribute it to local shops during my lunch break. The demand fa
surpassed our expectations and I soon found this exhausting and pleade
for HELP. The cereal master volunteered and lasted for a few sessions. H
soon decided to abandon our venture. I do miss our great product and ar
often stopped on the streets and asked to bring it back. I am offering, fc
the first time, our cereal recipes in Come Cook with Me.

Bailey's Creek Oat Cereal

cups rolled oats
cup sliced almonds
cup dried dates, chopped
cup dried, unsulfured apples, chopped
cup dried, unsulfured apricots, chopped

Mix all ingredients and store in airtight container.

Bailey's Creek Barley Cereal

4 cups rolled, whole barley
½ cup walnut pieces
½ cup dried pineapple, unsweetened, diced
½ cup dried papaya, unsulfured, diced
¼ cup Zante currants

Mix all ingredients and store in airtight container.

Bailey's Creek Rye Cereal

cups rolled, whole rye
cup pistachios, shelled
cup dried mango, unsulfured, diced
cup dried cranberries, apple sweetened, diced
cup dried blueberries

Mix all ingredients and store in airtight containers.

The Wheat and the Chaff

Why, why is it so difficult to separate the wheat and the chaff?

Does the id so override the ego that it renders one blind?

Unacceptable character flaws are buried deep in the chaff

Then suddenly strong Ivan travels from afar

Blows on the chaff and clearly reveals

A fruitless kernel, heretofore appearing as nutritious wheat…

After the storm and cleared of hidden disguises, the kernel presents...

Do I now post-Ivan follow a nutritious course or continue to munch on chaff

Please let me find wheat…

Pasta

Pasta With Lobster, Wild Mushrooms, and Cream

6 tablespoons butter
2 lobster tails
8 ounces shiitake mushrooms, stemmed, thinly sliced
½ cup (packed) thinly sliced fresh basil
6 green onions, thinly sliced
3 cloves garlic, chopped
1 ⅓ cups whipping cream
1 (8 ounce) bottle clam juice
12 ounces fettuccine
1/4 cup freshly grated Asiago cheese

Melt butter in heavy large skillet over medium-high heat. Add lobster tails and sauté until shells are bright red in spots, about 5 minutes. Cover skillet; reduce heat to low and cook until lobster is cooked through, about 6 minutes. Remove from heat. Using slotted spoon, transfer lobster to work surface. Using heavy large knife, cut each tail lengthwise in half. Remove meat from shell. Cut meat crosswise into ½ inch pieces. Return same skillet to medium-high heat (do not clean). Add mushrooms, half of basil, green onions, and garlic; sauté until mushrooms soften, about 5 minutes. Add cream and clam juice. Boil until sauce is slightly thickened, stirring occasionally, about 10 minutes. Reduce heat to low. Add lobster and simmer 1 minute. Stir in remaining basil. Season sauce to taste with salt and pepper. Meanwhile, cook pasta in large pot of boiling salted water until tender but still firm to the bite. Drain well. Return to pot. Pour sauce over pasta and add cheese; toss over low heat until warmed through, then serve. Yield: 4 servings
Note: This can be prepared with 1 ½ lbs shrimp instead of lobster, if you like.

Penne Puttanesca with Chicken

2 ounces penne rigate pasta
¼ pounds skinless boneless chicken thighs, cut into ½ inch pieces
(2 ounce) can anchovies, drained, oil reserved, chopped
garlic cloves, chopped
(28 ounce) can crushed tomatoes
cup pitted Kalamata olives, halved
¼ cup drained capers
½ teaspoon dried crushed red pepper
⅓ cup chopped fresh parsley

Cook pasta in large pot of boiling salted water until tender but still firm to bite, stirring occasionally. Drain.
Meanwhile, sprinkle chicken with salt and pepper. Heat reserved oil from anchovies in heavy large skillet over medium-high heat. Add chicken and chopped anchovies; sauté until chicken is no longer pink, about 3 minutes, stirring occasionally, about 5 minutes. Add parsley and drained pasta; stir to coat. Season with salt and pepper.

Shrimp, Kalamata, and Tomato Pasta

1 lb fresh shrimp
¼ cup lime juice
Tabasco
salt
2 tablespoons olive oil
2 cloves garlic, chopped
½ chili pepper, minced
1 tomato, chopped
Kalamata olives, chopped
1 tablespoon capers
½ cup white wine
1 (14-ounce) can chicken broth
1 tablespoon cornstarch
linguine or pasta of choice

Marinate shrimp for 2 hours in lime juice with salt and tabasco. Sauté garlic and pepper in olive oil. Combine tomatoes, olives, chili pepper and capers. Sauté for 2-3 minutes over low heat. Add wine and chicken broth. Thicken with cornstarch. Add the marinated shrimp and heat through. The shrimp are cooked by the lime juice during the two hours that they marinade, thus it is only necessary to heat them through when they are added to the sauce. Serve over linguine or pasta of choice (cooked according to package directions).

Betty Ruth's Spaghetti Sauce

2 pounds lean ground beef
1 pound Polish sausage, casing removed, chopped or sliced
3 large onions
4 bell peppers
4 cloves garlic
1 pound fresh mushrooms, sliced
1 small can dry Italian seasoning or 1½ tsps each of rosemary, basil,
     sage, oregano, thyme and marjoram)
½ cup dried parsley
2 tablespoons New Orleans Creole seasoning
salt
freshly ground black pepper to taste
4 bay leaves
4 quarts tomatoes
2 large cans tomato sauce
1 cup red wine
½ lb sharp cheddar (optional)

Sauté beef and sausage together in olive oil. Drain off drippings and set meat aside. Sauté vegetables in drippings and, again drain off excess drippings. With meats and vegetables in large pot, add tomatoes and mix well. Add tomato sauce and all seasonings. Simmer 2 to 3 hours. After 2 hours, add the grated cheddar and simmer for 2 to 3 hours longer. Freezes well.

Seafood Pasta

1 pound shrimp, lobster, or other seafood
3 tablespoons olive oil
2 teaspoon garlic, minced
⅓ cup lemon juice
2 teaspoon Dijon mustard
½ cup green, red, or yellow peppers, julienned
½ cup whole pitted olives
¼ cup grated Parmesan
1 teaspoon fresh dill weed minced or ½ teaspoon dry
1 cup green beans, thinly sliced
5 ounces linguini or other pasta of choice

Cut seafood into bite-size pieces; set aside. In medium saucepan, sauté
garlic in oil. Stir in lemon juice, Dijon and dill. Over low heat add beans
and peppers, simmer until tender. Add seafood, olives and Parmesan to
vegetable mixture. Cook linguini al dente. Top linguine with the sauce
Yield: 4 servings

Misnomer

Poetry is a misnomer.

The scribblings are prosaisms or emotion evoked thoughts.

Therefore, I am a prosaist.

I should not have raised your expectations.

In portraying myself as a writer of poetry!

Sandwiches

How to Make Tea Sandwiches

Suggested fillings:

Anchovy:
1 (3 ounce) package cream cheese
2 teaspoon anchovy paste
½ cup butter, creamed
1 teaspoon lemon juice
watercress of parsley, minced

Goat cheese and pecans:
2 (5 ½ ounces) logs soft fresh goat cheese (such as Montrachet)
1/2 cup chopped watercress leaves
5 tablespoons butter at room temperature
¾ cup finely chopped toasted pecans

Cucumber:
Cucumber slices
White wine vinegar
Butter

Thin slices of cucumber sprinkled with a little of white wine vinegar. Drain
in a sieve for about ½ hour. Drain away any excess liquid and pat dry with
a paper towel.

Tomato:
Tomato
Salt
Freshly ground pepper

Dip tomatoes in boiling water for a few seconds, slide skins off, pat dry with kitchen paper, slice tomatoes (thin) and arrange on slices of buttered bread. Season with a little freshly ground black pepper, cover with a second slice of bread.

Olive:
4 ounces cream cheese
watercress or parsley, minced
¼ cup chopped stuffed olives
1 teaspoon mayonnaise
2 tablespoons finely
chopped walnuts

Making sandwiches:
Allow 4 to 6 cut sandwich servings for each person. Choose the best-quality white or wheat bread as possible. Never serve end slices. Freezing the bread before cutting and then spreading makes for easier handling. Bread slices should be lightly buttered no matter what the filling. Unsalted butter should always be used. Butter should be at room temperature before spreading. Sandwiches will not become limp and soggy as readily if you spread the butter to the edge of the bread. Cut the crusts off the bread with a long, sharp knife after the sandwiches are filled. This keeps everything neater. Since tea sandwiches should be delicate, cut each sandwich in half on the diagonal or into thirds or fourths before serving. Decorative shapes can be made with cookie cutters.

My Tuna Melt

1 small can of tuna packed in water
½ onion, chopped
1 tablespoon Dijon or Wasabi mustard
1 dash tabasco sauce
½ teaspoon peppercorns packed in brine
1 slice whole wheat bread, toasted
2 slices fresh mozzarella cheese

Mix tuna, chopped onions, green peppercorns, tabasco and Dijon. Heat in microwave for 2 minutes. Place tuna mix on toast and top with mozzarella. Run under broiler until cheese is melted.

Sublimation And The Lonely Gourmand

When day is done and shadows fall, I dream of entering my therapeutic kitchen
and preparing a gourmet feast
I always prepare for at least two, subconsciously hoping that the phone will ring
and I'll not dine alone
99.9% of the time there is no call.
My best meals, as the one tonight, are devoured in solitude
99.8% of the time I am a glutton and consume the dinner prepared for me and
the "wished for" friend
Night after night, my cup runneth over and I leave the table culinarily satiated.

Breads & Pastries

Basic Mix for Bread Machines

11 cups flour
½ cup sugar (optional)
2 teaspoons salt
½ cup powdered buttermilk

Final ingredients:
1 cup warm water
1 egg
2 tablespoons butter
3 ½ cups bread mix
1 ½ teaspoons yeast

Combine dry ingredients (except yeast) and store in an airtight container.
When ready to use, add final ingredients (yeast, butter, water, and egg) to
3 ½ cups of the bread mix and bake.
Yield: 3 loaves of bread
Note: You can use flour of choice. When I use wheat or rye, I increase the
yeast, ½ to 1 teaspoon. I also like to add a handful of Harvest Grain Blend
to the dry mix. My source is King Arthur Flours:
http://www.kingarthurflour.com/

Earthy Multigrain Bread

¾ cup water
1 tablespoon butter, softened
1 teaspoon salt
2 tablespoons sunflower seed
1 tablespoon sesame seed
1 tablespoon flax seed
1 tablespoon millet
1 tablespoon quinoa
1 cup bread flour
1 cup whole wheat flour
1 tablespoon dry milk powder
¼ cup packed brown sugar
4 ½ teaspoons bread machine yeast

Preheat oven 350° F. Place ingredients in the pan of the bread machine in the order recommended by the manufacturer. Select cycle; press Start. This bread is a solid textured loaf appropriate for sandwiches, spreads, or eating with a meal. It has two kinds of grains and three kinds of seeds in it. It is solid and hardy, yet light and sweet. Bake for 45-60 minutes. Yield: 2 servings. Note: I often use my bread machine only for kneading and partial rising, then I form loaf and bake it in the oven.

Cheese Biscuits

2 cups flour
2 teaspoon baking powder
½ teaspoon salt
1 cup Parmesan, grated
¼ cup butter

Sift flour, baking powder and salt together. Add Parmesan. Cut the butter into the flour mixture with a pastry blender or fork. Stir in milk with fork, ¾ cup or enough to make soft dough. Knead 30 seconds. Roll ¼ inch thick. Cut with 2 inch cookie cutter. Put on buttered baking sheet. Bake 12 to 15 minutes at 450° F.

Cranberry Orange Biscuits

2 cups Bisquick
1 tablespoon grated orange rind
½ cup chopped walnuts
½ cup sugar
1 egg
¼ cup orange juice
1 (8 ounce) can whole cranberry suace

Preheat oven to 400°. Stir together Bisquick, grated orange rind, and nuts. Mix egg, orange juice, and cranberries. Add this mixture to dry ingredients. Stir until just moistened. Roll out dough to about ⅛ to ¼ and cut with a 2 inch biscuit cutter. Bake 25 minutes, or until golden brown. Yield: 12 servings

Easy Cinnamon Rolls

2 (8 ounce) cans refrigerated crescent rolls
6 tablespoons butter
⅓ cup firmly packed brown sugar
¼ cup chopped pecans
1 tablespoon sugar
1 teaspoon cinnamon
⅔ cup powdered sugar
1 tablespoon milk
¼ teaspoon vanilla
⅛ tablespoon salt

Unroll crescent rolls, and separate each dough portion along center perforation to form 4 rectangles: press diagonal perforations to seal. Stir together butter, pecans, brown sugar, sugar and cinnamon; spread evenly over one side of each rectangle. Roll up jelly roll fashion, starting at long end. Gently cut each log into 6 (1 inch thick) slices, using a serrated knife. Place rolls ¼ inch apart, into 2 greased cake pans.
Bake at 375° for 15 to 18 minutes or until golden. Cool 5 to 10 minutes. Stir together powdered sugar, milk, vanilla and salt. Drizzle over warm rolls.

Dried Fruit Scones

cups unbleached plain or pastry flour

tablespoon baking powder

⁄4 teaspoon salt

⁄3 cup sugar

⁄4 cup butter

large eggs (one separated)

⁄8 teaspoon citrus oil

⁄2 cup dried fruit (of choice)

⁄4 cup buttermilk or yogurt (may need more)

Preheat oven to 450°. In a large bowl, mix the flour, baking powder, salt, and sugar. Cut butter as you would for pie crust or biscuits. Stir in 1 whole egg and yolk, the extract, and fruit, then add buttermilk or yogurt until mixture holds together (mix only as much as necessary). Transfer to well-floured surface and pat out into a 1½ thick rectangle. Using a bowl scraper or pizza wheel, cut into 3 inch squares, then cut each square in half to form triangles. Place scones on a lightly greased or parchment lined baking sheet. Whisk the reserved egg white until foamy; add ¼ tsp of the extract. Brush tops of scones with beaten egg white and sprinkle with sugar. Bake scones in 450° oven for 10 to 15 minutes, or until lightly browned. Remove from oven and cool completely on a wire rack.

Elmira's Cornbread

1 ½ cups water ground cornmeal
½ teaspoon salt
1 teaspoon baking powder
buttermilk
¼ teaspoon soda
1 ½ cups cracklings (optional)
3 tablespoons bacon drippings
1 egg

Mix dry ingredients. Make well and break egg into meal mix, stir. Add enough buttermilk to make a soft (almost liquid) batter. Put bacon drippings in iron skillet and place in oven until it begins to smoke. Pour about 2 tablespoons of the hot drippings into cornbread mixture, stir in and pour mixture into hot skillet. Bake in 475°F oven for 15 minutes or until well set. If not brown enough, run under broiler for a bit. (To make crackling bread, add 1 ½ cups cracklings to batter). Note: Coarse, water ground cornmeal is available from the store at Callaway Gardens: www.callawaygardens.com/Callaway/info/things.shop.aspx

Granola Banana-Nut Bread

 stick butter
 cup brown sugar, packed
 eggs
 cup buttermilk
 bananas, mashed
 cup flour
 teaspoon baking powder
 teaspoon soda
 cups crushed granola
 cup chopped pecans

Preheat oven to 350°. Cream butter and sugar. Add eggs, one at a time and beat well. Mix buttermilk and bananas and reserve. Mix flour, baking powder, soda, and salt. Alternate mixing flour and banana mixtures into sugar/butter/egg mixture. Mix the granola and nuts. Fold into the original mixture. Bake in greased and floured loaf pans 45 to 60 minutes.

Herb Bread

2 ⅓ cups bread flour
1 tablespoon dry milk
1 teaspoon salt
2 tablespoons parsley
1 tablespoon caraway seeds
1 tablespoon dill
1 tablespoon butter
2 tablespoons honey
1 cup water
1 teaspoon dry yeast

Add ingredients to bread maker in the order recommended by the manufacturer. Push Start, and the bread will be ready in four hours!
I often use my bread machine only for kneading and partial rising, then form a loaf and bake it in the oven (30 to 40 minutes at 350º F).
Note: I like to prepare individual zip lock bags of all the dry ingredient ahead and store them. When ready to bake, add the butter, water, and honey.

Spoon Bread

2 cups milk
1 cup cornmeal
1 teaspoon salt
4 tablespoons butter
4 eggs, separated

Pour the milk into the upper part of a double boiler and cook over hot water until the milk almost reaches a boil. Add the cornmeal slowly, stirring constantly. Continue cooking and stirring until the mixture is thick and smooth. This should take only about 1 minute. Do not let the mixture get too thick. Add the salt and butter and remove from the heat to cool slightly. Beat the egg yolks until light and yellow and add to the cornmeal. Beat the egg whites until stiff but not dry and carefully fold into the cornmeal. Pour into a well-buttered casserole and bake in a 375° F oven 35-40 minutes, or until well puffed and browned on top. Serve from the casserole and pass butter, salt, and freshly ground black pepper. Yield: serves 6

Paper Thin Cornbread

¾ cup yellow cornmeal
1 cup boiling water
½ teaspoon salt
3 tablespoons butter

Preheat oven to 400º. Stir cornmeal into boiling water until smooth. Add
salt and melted butter. Stir again. Spread very thinly onto ungreased cooki
sheet. Bake until crisp and browning, about 30 minutes. To serve, break
into odd shaped pieces and serve warm. Note: Reduce fat by substituting
yogurt for butter.

Zucchini Nut Bread

cups zucchini

eggs

cup salad oil

/2 cups sugar

teaspoon lemon rind, grated

/2 cups flour

teaspoon baking soda

teaspoons baking powder

teaspoon ginger

teaspoon nutmeg

teaspoon salt

cup pecans

red zucchini with shredding blade of processor; drain and set aside. ace eggs, oil, sugar and lemon rind in container and blend. Sift dry gredients together and add, one cup at a time, to oil mixture. Blend only til flour disappears. Remove from container and fold in zucchini shreds d nut pieces. Spoon into small, greased loaf pans and bake in 350° F en for 30 to 45 minutes. Let cool in pan.

Janie's Ice Box Rolls

2 ½ cups boiling water
2 tablespoons shortening, heaping
¾ cup sugar
2 cakes yeast
¼ cup lukewarm water
2 eggs, beaten lightly
8 cups bread flour
1 tablespoon salt
melted butter

Mix boiling water, ½ cup sugar, and shortening together; cool un
lukewarm. Soften yeast in lukewarm water. Add 1 teaspoon of sugar a
stir into the first mixture. Add beaten eggs, then stir in 4 cups flour. M
thoroughly. Stir in 4 more cups flour. Mix thoroughly. Not necessary
knead. Brush top of dough with melted butter and cover tightly. Store
refrigerator until ready to use. Dough will keep for 1 week to 10 da
in refrigerator. When you are ready to bake them, shape rolls and put
warm place until they are double in bulk. Bake in 425° F oven for abc
8 minutes.

Pate Brisee II

cups all purpose flour
egg
tablespoons chilled butter
tablespoons ice water
teaspoon salt

ace all ingredients, except ice water, in food processor. Process until the
ixture has consistency of coarse meal. With the machine still running,
d ice water (1 ½ to 2 tbsp) to processor. Stop just before it forms a ball.
frigerate at least 30 minutes before using. Yield: two 8 inch crusts

Graham Glover's Biscuits

2 big tablespoons self-rising flour
1 tablespoon Crisco
buttermilk to mix

Cut Crisco into flour with pastry blender or fork. Add buttermilk and mi
Pat or roll out. Cut with biscuit cutter. Bake 5 to 10 minutes at 450° F
475° F.

Kneading, Kneeling and Needing

As a child I nightly knelt at my bedside
I offered my perfunctory prayer, "Now I lay me down to sleep,
I pray the lord my soul to keep"
ow in my dotage, as I knead or kneel, the prayer is no longer perfunctory
I earnestly pray that my soul shall rise as a well baked loaf.

Desserts

Baked Grapefruit Alaska

medium grapefruit
cup granulated sugar
10 ounce) jar orange marmalade
egg whites, room temperature
wdered sugar

t each grapefruit in half. With a grapefruit knife, remove center core
m each half. To remove membrane, cut around between the flesh and
pith to completely detach flesh from shell. Slip the knife down each
le of membranes, between grapefruit sections. Remove all membranes
d seeds, leaving flesh in grapefruit shell. Place on a baking sheet. Place
rmalade in a small saucepan. Heat until warm. In a medium bowl,
at egg whites until soft peaks form - Slowly beat in granulated sugar 1
lespoon at a time. Continue beating until stiff. Carefully fold in warm
rmalade. Cover grapefruit in shells with meringue, bringing meringue
the edge of the shells. Filled shells may stand at room temperature 2 to
ours until ready to use.

t before serving, preheat oven to 425° F. Bake grapefruit 8 to 9
nutes or until nicely browned. Sprinkle with powdered sugar and serve
mediately.

rvings: 6

Basic Meringues

4 egg whites, at room temperature
¼ teaspoon cream of tartar or 1 teaspoon vinegar
pinch of salt
1 teaspoon vanilla
1 cup powdered sugar

Combine egg whites, cream of tartar, salt, and vanilla in a large bo̶w̶l
Beat at low speed until eggs begin to foam, then at medium speed un̶til
egg whites hold soft peaks. Gradually add ¾ cup sugar, 1 tablespoon a̶t̶ a̶
time, while beating on high speed. Beat until meringue is very stiff, d̶ry
and no longer grainy. Gently fold in remaining sugar. Meringues sho̶uld
be dried rather than baked to obtain proper texture. Shape meringue̶s̶ in̶to
desired sizes. Place in a preheated 200° F oven for 1 hour. Turn heat o̶ff
and let meringues remain in oven at least 4 hours or overnight. Wh̶en
completely dry, meringues may be kept covered in a dry airy place f̶or
several weeks or they may be frozen. If frozen, uncover to thaw and pl̶ace
in oven on very low heat if they feel moist in any way. Makes 12 tarts, 2̶4
tartlets, 1 pie shell or 3 meringue discs. Yield: 12 servings

Bananas Foster

¼ cup sliced almonds
 tablespoons unsalted butter
 tablespoons light brown sugar
½ teaspoon cinnamon
 inch of fresh ground nutmeg
 inch of salt
 teaspoon grated orange zest
¼ cup banana liquor
¼ cup orange liquor (Grand Marnier)
⅛ cup amaretto
½ cup dark rum (Myers)
 small bananas sliced lengthwise
 scoops vanilla ice cream

 oast almonds lightly in a skillet and set aside. Melt butter in flambé pan
 r large skillet, then add brown sugar cinnamon, nutmeg, orange zest, and
 alt. Cook until well mixed. Put in the bananas and sauté until they begin
 o turn soft, pour in banana liquor, orange liquor, amaretto, and half of the
 um. Heat the remainder of the rum in a small saucepan until boiling. Pour
 um over bananas and ignite with a long match (Pan should be removed
 rom flame before adding alcohol). Shake pan and spoon liquid over
 he bananas until flames go out. Serve over ice cream. Sprinkle toasted
 lmonds over top. Yield: 4 servings
 Contributor: Herman King

Blackberry (Jelly-Roll) Cobbler

½ cup butter
1 cup sugar
1 cup water
1 ½ cups self rising flour
½ cup butter
⅓ cup milk, room temp
2 cups blackberries
1 teaspoon cinnamon
2 tablespoons sugar

Melt ½ cup butter in a long, round, or oval baking dish; set aside. Heat sugar and water until sugar melts, set aside. Make cobbler dough by butter into flour until particles are like fine crumbs. Add milk and with a fork until dough leaves sides of bowl. Turn out on floured board and knead 3 or 4 times. Roll out into 11 x 9 inch x ¼ inch rectangle. Sprinkle berries over dough, sprinkle with cinnamon and roll up like a jelly roll and cut into 1-½ inch slices. Carefully place in dish over melted butter, pour sugar syrup carefully around slices (crust will absorb liquid). Bake for 45 minutes. Sprinkle 2 tablespoons sugar over crust and bake for 15 minutes longer. Serve warm or cold.

Brandied Orange Bombe

cup white seedless raisins
cups brandy
½ quarts orange sherbet
½ quarts vanilla ice cream, slightly softened
cup toasted slivered
monds
arnish: fresh mint or orange zest

oak raisins in brandy in a covered jar for 12 to 72 hours at room temperature.
hill a 2-quart mold in the freezer. Spread inside of mold with orange
erbet or sorbet, making layer about ½ inch thick. Put the mold back
to the freezer and prepare the vanilla ice cream as follows. Drain the
isins and stir them, along with almonds, into softened ice cream without
tting ice cream melt. Pack ice cream into center of mold. Cover the mold
ith lid, or with foil. Return to freezer and freeze at least 6 hours. To
imold, remove the cover or foil, then place the mold on a chilled serving
ate, wipe the outside of the mold several times with a cloth wrung out
hot water and lift the mold. The bombe can be unmolded ahead and
ept frozen until serving time. Garnish bombe with sprig of fresh mint or
ange zest.

Pecan Tassies

1 ½ recipes Pâté Brisee-II (*see recipe page 327)
1 ½ cups chopped pecans
1 cup sugar
1 stick butter
3 large eggs, beaten
½ teaspoon lemon juice
1 teaspoon vanilla
1 dash salt
1 cup light Karo syrup

Make Pâté Brisee and thinly line tiny tartlet (1 to 1 ½ inches) tins. Brown
butter in saucepan until golden brown-DO NOT BURN, let cool. In separate
bowl add other ingredients in order listed, mixing after each addition. Add
cooled butter last and spoon into unbaked tartlet shell. Bake for 25 minutes
in 350° F oven. Cool in tins on racks, loosen with tip and turn out on
rack to cool completely. To make a pecan pie, pour into unbaked pie shell
and bake at 425° F for minutes, then lower temperature to 325° F for
minutes. Yield 8 dozen tassies or 1 pie.
Note: Pecan tassies freeze well and are great to pull out for picnics!

Elmira's Basic Cake Layers

1 cup butter
2 cups sugar
3 cups flour
1 teaspoon vanilla flavoring
8 egg whites

Cream butter and sugar. Add vanilla to butter and sugar. Gradually stir in flour. Beat egg whies until stiff and fold into mixture. Cook layers at 450° F for 10 to 15 minutes in hot oven, (cook until they do not shake in the middle or until inserted toothpick comes out clean!).
Note: Elmira cooked her cake layers fast in a very hot oven, this method did not allow them to dry out.

Heavenly Hash

25 marshmallows
25 candied cherries
1 pint whipping cream
1 cup pecans
sherry
1 cup fresh coconut, grated
2 teaspoons powdered sugar

Cut each marshmallow into four pieces. Slice cherries, saving a few to decorate top. Mix marshmallows with cream and let stand an hour or more and then whip stiff. Mix in cherries, nuts, coconut, and powdered sugar. Flavor with sherry. Put in refrigerator to chill and set.

Note: This was an old standby for Sunday dinners at my Grandmother Janie's, served after fried chicken, rice and gravy, etc.

No calorie counters in those days!

Ambrosia

cups fresh orange sections
cup fresh coconut, grated

ix and chill.

Glazed Fruit Tartlets

For tartlet shells:
¼ lb butter, softened
½ cup sugar
1 egg yolk
½ cup sugar
dash salt
1 teaspoon vanilla extract
1 tablespoon grated orange rind
1 tablespoon orange juice
1 ¾ cups flour

For glaze:
½ cup sugar
1 ½ tablespoons cornstarch
dash salt
1 cup orange juice
2 teaspoons grated orange peel
1 tablespoon orange-flavored liqueur
4 cups fruit: kiwi, Mandarin oranges, grapes, strawberries, etc.

Preheat oven to 350º F. In a medium bowl, beat butter until fluffy. Do not use processor. Gradually mix in sugar, beating until light. Add egg yolk, orange juice, vanilla, and orange peel. Mix in flour. Press dough into tartlet molds. Bake 10 to 15 minutes or until lightly browned. Cool in molds 1 minutes. Insert tip of knife between edge of crust and mold. Invert in your hand. Cool completely on racks. If frozen, you will need to crisp in a warm oven.
Prepare orange glaze: mix sugar, cornstarch, and salt in a small saucepan. Gradually stir in orange juice until smooth. Heat to boiling, stirring

onstantly. Boil and stir 2 minutes. Add orange peel. Cover and cool. Stir
n orange liqueur.

ill tartlet with desired fruit, one type per tart. Carefully spoon orange
laze over top, covering fruit completely. May be prepared ahead and
efrigerated up to 8 hours before serving.

I Forgot Dessert

1 quart chocolate ice cream (or frozen yogurt)
¼ cup crème de menthe
chocolate shavings or sprig of mint
¼ cup crème de cocoa

Place ice cream and liqueurs in blender; buzz. Serve in small brandy
snifter. Garnish with chocolate shavings or a sprig of mint. Place a cookie
or profiterole on plate (optional).
Note: I always stay a 'quart ahead' in my freezer after a near disaster during
a dinner party when I realized that I had completely forgotten dessert.
was saved by chocolate ice milk -necessity was the mother of invention!

Crackoos

2 ½ cups Bailey's Creek Cereal (*see recipe page 297)
¼ cup flour
1 teaspoon salt
¾ teaspoon cinnamon
¼ teaspoon nutmeg
¼ cup honey
2 egg whites
¼ cup canola oil

Mix all dry ingredients, then work in honey and oil. Drop by teaspoonfuls onto cookie sheet and bake for 12-15 minutes at 350° F.

Pumpkin Cheesecake

2 tablespoons butter, softened
⅓ cup gingersnap crumbs
4 (8 ounce) packages cream cheese, room temp
1 ½ cups dark brown sugar, packed
5 eggs
1 (16 ounce) can pumpkin puree
1 teaspoon cinnamon
1 teaspoon allspice
¼ teaspoon ginger
¼ cup plain flour
¼ teaspoon salt
maple syrup

Pecan topping:
1 cup chopped pecans
1 tablespoons brown sugar
1 tablespoons butter
3 tablespoons flour
toasted pecan halves for garnish
whipped cream (optional)

1. Generously butter a 9 inch spring form pan with softened butter. Sprinkle the gingersnap crumbs into the pan and shake to coat the bottom and sides evenly.
2. Preheat oven to 325º F. In a large bowl beat the cream cheese with a wooden spoon until fluffy. Gradually beat in the brown sugar. Add eggs, one at a time, mixing well after each addition. Sift in the dry ingredients. Blend well. Beat in the pumpkin puree. Pour the batter into prepared pan.
3. Bake in the center of the oven 1 ½ to 1 ¾ hours, until the cake pulls

away from the sides of the pan and toothpick inserted in the center comes out clean. Remove from oven and cool on rack 1 hour. Carefully remove the ring from the springform and let the cake finish cooling at room temperature. Refrigerate, covered, until chilled.

4. Brush the top of the cake with maple syrup and garnish with toasted pecan halves.

5. Mix pecans with brown sugar, butter and flour to make crusty topping, bake for 15 minutes longer.

6. Serve with whipped cream, if desired. (Add ginger to whipped cream topping for an added touch).

Lizzies

3 cups seedless raisins
½ cup bourbon
1 ½ cups flour
1 teaspoon soda
1 ½ teaspoons cinnamon
½ teaspoon nutmeg
½ teaspoon ground cloves
¼ cup butter, softened
½ cup light brown sugar
2 eggs
1 ½ pounds candied fruit (fruitcake mix)
4 cups pecan pieces

Mix raisins and bourbon, let stand 1 hr or overnight. Sift together and reserve: flour, soda, cinnamon, nutmeg, and cloves. Beat butter, eggs, and brown sugar together until light and fluffy. Beat in flour mixture, beating until smooth. Stir in raisins, fruit, and nuts. Drop from spoon onto greased cookie sheets (I keep my fingers wet and press each dollop together well). Bake at 325º F 25 to 30 minutes or until firm. Remove and cool completely on wire rack. Yield: 6-7 dozen
Note: I rarely have any left, but, have found that they freeze well and keep forever. Stash them in a baggie for 2:00 am freezer raids.....

Bird Nest Cookies

¼ cup brown sugar
1 cup pecans, chopped
½ cup butter
guava jelly
1 egg yolk
1 cup flour
1 egg white

Cream butter and sugar. Add egg yolk, then one cup of flour. Form small balls (tsp size), dip in egg white, then roll in chopped nuts. Press centers to indent and bake in 350º oven for 8 minutes. Remove and press centers again and return to oven for 10 minutes. Using a teaspoon, fill centers with guava jelly.

Tony's Creole Custard Flan

1 cup cream
1 cup milk
1 teaspoon vanilla
3 eggs
2 egg yolks
1 cup sugar
¼ cup water
6 teaspoon crushed almonds

Scald milk and cream in pot, add vanilla. Combine the eggs, egg yolks and ½ cup sugar; beat until well blended. Gradually pour milk into egg mixture, stirring constantly. In a heavy skillet, heat the remaining sugar over moderate heat until it is melted. Gradually add water and boil until well-blended and brown. Pour this caramel equally into 6 custard cups. Sprinkle 1 teaspoon crushed almonds into each cup. When it sets, pour custard into each cup and place them in a pan of hot water. Bake in moderate oven 45 minutes or until knife comes out clean. Cool. When cold, unmold onto serving dishes. You may use single large mold instead of individual cups. Serves 6.

Quick Chocolate Pots de Crème

envelope unflavored gelatin

cup cold water

(6 ounce) package semi-sweet chocolate bits

tablespoons sugar

teaspoon salt

cup milk, scalded

cup crushed ice

egg yolks

cup whipping cream

½ teaspoon vanilla or 2 teaspoon crème de menthe

ombine water and gelatin in blender container; mix and let stand 2 minutes. dd chocolate bits, sugar, and salt. Add hot milk; blend until chocolate nelted and mixture smooth, 15 to 20 seconds. Add ice, egg, cream and anilla. Blend until ice melts, about 20 seconds. Yield: 8 servings

Lemon Curd

4 eggs
4 egg yolks
4 tablespoons grated lemon peels
½ pound butter
2 cups sugar
8 tablespoons lemon juice

Place eggs and yolks in double boiler and mix gently; add remainir
ingredients. Cook over simmering water stirring with a wooden spoc
until thickened. Store covered in refrigerator. Use with recipe for lemc
curd tartlets or Pâté Brisee II (*see recipes page 351 and 327).

Lemon Curd Tartlets

 pound butter, softened
 cup sugar
egg yolk
tablespoons lemon juice
¾ cups flour
tablespoon grated lemon rind
recipe Lemon Curd (*see recipe page 350)

reheat oven to 350° F. In a medium bowl, beat butter until fluffy. Do
ot use processor. Gradually mix in sugar, beating until light. Add egg
olk, lemon juice, vanilla, and lemon peel. Mix in flour. Press into tartlet
olds. Bake for 15 to 20 minutes or until lightly browned. Cool in molds
) minutes. Insert knife tip between crust and mold and gently invert into
ind. Cool completely on racks. May be frozen.

Lemon Bisque

1 package lemon Jello
1 ¼ cups graham cracker crumbs
2 tablespoons brown sugar
2 tablespoons white sugar
⅛ teaspoon salt
1 teaspoon cinnamon
2 tablespoons butter
1 ¼ cups chopped pecans
1 can (8-ounce) Carnation milk, very cold
1 lemon rind, grated
3 tablespoons lemon juice

Prepare Jello and chill until like syrup. Prepare crumbs, sugar, brown sugar, cinnamon, and butter by rubbing together; set aside. Beat the can of Carnation milk till thick; add juice and rind of lemon, then add the Jello. Spread half of crumbs in 13 inch x 10 ½ inch pan, pour in Jello mixture and put rest of crumbs on top. Refrigerate. Yield: 6 servings

Old English Plum Pudding

cups currants
cups raisins
cup candied orange peel
tablespoons ground ginger
cup sugar
teaspoon ground cloves
teaspoon ground allspice
teaspoon nutmeg
teaspoon cinnamon
½ cups light brown sugar
cup almonds, chopped
cups fine bread crumbs
lb beef suet, ground
½ cups tart apples, unpeeled
eggs, well beaten
¼ cups milk
cup dark rum
cup butter
tablespoons brandy
cups unbleached, plain flour

In a very large mixing bowl, combine the dried fruit, candied peel, nuts, brown sugar, flour, spices, bread crumbs, suet, and apples. Mix with hands until well-blended. In another smaller mixing bowl, combine eggs, milk, and rum. Add to dry mixture and mix well. The pudding may be steamed in the traditional 1 ½ qt pudding molds which come with their own lids, or in any desired container, such as aluminum cans and deep Jello molds. In any case, be sure the mold is well buttered. To be assured that the steamed pudding will slip out with ease, butter the mold thoroughly and liberally, then refrigerate for about 20 minutes. Butter again before spooning the pudding mixture into the mold. Fill each mold about ⅔ full, cover with a lid or tightly with foil. Place covered molds on a rack in several deep kettles. Add 2 inches of boiling water to each kettle. Cover kettles and steam puddings, adding additional water as necessary, until toothpick inserted comes out clean, or about 1 ½ hours. Next, place covered mold in a 200° F oven for about 8 hours or overnight. Store in heavy foil in dark place to mature (puddings will keep for at least a year if they last that long!). Serve in thin slices at room temperature, or warm, steamed again in the same manner for about 1 ½ hours. Either way, serve with cold brandy butter.

Brandy butter: cream the sugar and butter, add brandy a few drops at the time, and beat until fluffy. Chill. Serve cold. Serves 8-10.

Old Fashion Gingerbread

½ cup butter
½ cup sugar
2 eggs
½ cup molasses
1 ½ cups cake flour
1 teaspoon ginger
1 teaspoon allspice
1 teaspoon cinnamon
1 tsp soda
½ cup buttermilk
Topping (optional):
2 teaspoon cinnamon
½ cup brown sugar
¼ cup flour
1 cup pecans, chopped
¼ cup butter

In a bowl cream butter and sugar. Add eggs, beating well. Blend in molasses. In a separate bowl, combine flour, spices, and soda. Fold flour into mixture. Add buttermilk. Bake in 350° until fork done. Serve with Lemon and Raisin Sauce (*see recipe page 277).
Optional Topping: Blend together all ingredients until crumbly. Spread generously over cake. Return to oven for 5 minutes.

Meringues with Ice Cream and Strawberries

6 egg whites
½ teaspoon cream of tartar
1 ½ cups superfine sugar
1 teaspoon vanilla
strawberries

Separate eggs while cold, but allow them to come to room temperature before beating. Beat egg whites at high speed of mixer adding cream of tartar. Continue to beat for about 15 minutes gradually adding sugar, two tablespoons at a time, along with vanilla. Spoon onto cookie sheets lined with aluminum foil that has been sprayed with oil. Spoon out enough to make 10 (4 inch diameter) circles, using back of spoon make a nest in center of each. Bake at 275° for 45 minutes, then turn oven off and let stand in oven for one hour. Cool completely and remove very carefully by peeling foil from bottom of meringues. Can be made the day before and stored in airtight containers. Serve with vanilla ice cream in the middle of the meringue and fresh strawberries on top. Yield: 10 servings

Chocolate Chess Pie

½ cups sugar
½ tablespoons cocoa
cup pecans, chopped
teaspoon vanilla
whole eggs
small can evaporated milk
sh salt
 stick butter, melted
recipe Pâté Brisee II (*see recipe page 327) for pie crust

ix sugar and cocoa with spoon only. Add other ingredients and pour
to shell and bake 10 minutes at 375°. Decrease heat to 300° and bake 35
inutes or until set. Freezes well. Serve with ice cream.
ote: Can be baked in custard cup without pastry and topped with ice
eam or whipped cream.

Chocolate Mousse Cake

7 ounce semi-sweet chocolate
¼ pound unsalted butter
7 eggs, separated
1 cup sugar
1 teaspoon vanilla
⅛ teaspoon cream of tartar
½ pint whipping cream
⅓ cup powdered sugar
Chocolate Leaves (*see recipe page 359)

Preheat oven to 325°. In a small saucepan, melt chocolate and butter ov
low heat. In a large bowl, beat egg yolks and ¾ cup sugar until very lig
and fluffy, about 5 minutes. Gradually beat in warm chocolate mixture a
vanilla.

In another large bowl, beat egg whites with cream of tartar until sc
peaks form. Add remaining ¼ cup sugar, 1 tablespoon at a time. Contin
beating until stiff. Fold egg whites carefully into chocolate mixture. Po
3/4 of the batter into an ungreased 9 inch x 3 inch springform pan. Cov
remaining batter and refrigerate. Bake cake 35 minutes. Remove ca
from oven and cool. Cake will drop as it cools. Remove outside ring
springform pan. Stir refrigerated batter to soften slightly. Spread on top
cake. Refrigerate until firm.

Prepare whipped cream frosting - in a small bowl, beat whipping crea
until soft peaks form. Add powdered sugar and vanilla. Beat until sti
Place chocolate leaves around sides or on top off frosting.

Chocolate Leaves

non-poisonous leaves, camellia or rose
ounce semisweet chocolate

ne baking sheet with waxed paper. Melt chocolate over hot water or in
icrowave. Wash and dry leaves. Spread chocolate with small spatula on
derside of leaves. Place chocolate side up on waxed paper and chill.
ay be frozen (before detaching from leaf or after).

Chocolate leaves

Gingersnap Crust with Lemon Ice Cream

35 gingersnaps
¼ pound butter, melted
1 tablespoon powdered sugar
1 quart lemon ice cream

Crumb gingersnaps; add melted butter and sugar; mix well. Press into p
tin and bake for 5 minutes at 300º. Cool. Freezes well! Fill with lemon i
cream.

Miss Maude's Caramel Icing

½ cups sugar

cup milk

stick butter

inch paraffin

tablespoons karo

cup sugar

ilk (optional)

ix 2 ½ cups sugar, milk, butter, paraffin and Karo in a heavy saucepan
r well until mixed and bring to a boil over medium heat. Cook slowly.
eanwhile brown ½ cup sugar in an iron skillet, to a deep golden brown.
ur browned sugar into boiling mixture. It should be ready at this point
ou can check for a soft ball (to check for a soft ball, you drop about ¼
spoon in a cup of water and feel it to see if it has cooked enough to form
soft ball!). Remove from heat and set aside to cool a little. Add vanilla
d beat until ready to spread on cake. If it gets too hard before you can
t it spread on cake, add a little hot milk or ½ and ½.

ote: I make two recipes of Elmira's Basic Cake Layers (*see recipe page
7) and split each layer to make a 7-layer caramel cake. If making a
layer cake, you will need to make 2 recipes of the icing.

ntributor: "Miss" Maude Beeland Pipes

English Summer Pudding

14 slices white bread, crusts trimmed
4 cups mixed berries (blackberries and raspberries)
⅓ cup sugar
3 tablespoons water
Mock Devonshire Cream (see recipe page 279)

Line a charlotte mold (or any 8-inch bowl) with plastic wrap so that y
have enough overhang to cover the finished mold. Place one whole slice
bread in the bottom of bowl. Arrange halved slices of bread, overlappi
them, around sides of mold and press the bread, covering bottom and si
of bowl. In a saucepan, combine the berries, water and sugar and bring
a simmer over moderate heat. Stir for about three minutes, until the berr
are crushed and the sugar dissolved. Remove pan from the heat and
mixture cool. Drain the berries, reserving the juice. Spoon one third of
berries into the mold and top it with enough of the remaining bread,
into pieces, to cover the berries layer. Repeat these layers twice, end
with a bread layer. Pour a little of the reserved juice over the mold. P
plastic wrap over the mold. Cover the mold with a round of waxed pa
cut to fit the inside of the mold. Top the waxed paper with a plate or s
cardboard cut to fit the inside of the mold, and weight the pudding eve
with a two pound weight or with a few cans from pantry. Chill the pudd
overnight (or at least four hours). Just before serving, remove the weig
the plate or cardboard. Invert the pudding onto a chilled platter and remc
the plastic wrap. Heat the reserved berry juice until reduced by half. Se
the juice and Mock Devonshire with the sliced pudding. Serves 8-10.

English Summer Pudding

Elmira's Lane Cake

Cake layers
1 cup butter
2 cups sugar
3 cups flour
8 egg whites

Icing:
8 egg yolks
2 cups sugar
1 cup white raisins
1 cup pecans
2 cups fresh coconut
½ cup bourbon

Cream butter and sugar. Add vanilla to butter and sugar. Gradually stir
flour. Beat egg whites until stiff and foldinto mixture. Cook layers at 45
for 10 to 15 minutes in hot oven, so they will not dry out (until they do r
shake in the middle).

To make icing:
Mix egg yolks and sugar, cook over low heat until thickened. Add raisi
pecans, and coconut. Add bourbon last. Spread between layers and ice t
top.

Kahlúa, Fudge, and Macadamia Pie

cups vanilla wafer crumbs, fine

cup wheat germ

cup butter, melted

quart vanilla ice cream

tablespoons Kahlúa

cup macadamia nuts, coarsely chopped

jar chocolate fudge sauce (such as Smucker's)

ombine vanilla wafer crumbs, wheat germ, and melted butter, reserve ½ up of mix. Press evenly Into a 9 inch pie pan. Bake for 4 minutes at 325°. ool. Mix softened ice cream with Kahlúa and macadamias, freeze 30 inutes. Spread fudge over ice cream layer. Top with reserved ½ cup of astry mix. Freeze until serving time.

Pecan Pralines

1 cup sugar
1 cup (packed) light brown sugar
3 tablespoons butter
2/3 cup sweetened condensed milk
1 ½ tablespoons vanilla
1 ½ cup pecan pieces

Combine everything except the vanilla and pecans in a heavy saucepan over medium heat. Stir with a wooden spoon as you cook, being very careful not to splash. Scrape down the sides of the pan for any sugar granules that may get up there. When the mixture turns translucent, add the pecans and the vanilla. Continue to cook and stir. The mixture will begin to brown slowly. The whole trick to making good pralines--and it is tricky--is to get them off the heat at the right point. The reading you should see on the candy thermometer should be the "soft ball" temperature, about 235*. It will take about 15 to 20 minutes. With a large spoon, drop some of the praline mixture onto a cookie sheet, waxed paper, or a marble slab, making discs about two inches across. Allow to cool. Remove with a very thin spatula and wrap tightly. Makes 16-20 pralines

Pecan Tassies

for pastry:
cups all purpose flour
egg
) tablespoons chilled butter
tablespoons ice water
teaspoon salt

lace all ingredients, except ice water, in food processor. Process until the
ixture has consistency of coarse meal. With the machine still running,
ld ice water (1 ½ to 2 tbsp) to processor. Stop just before it forms a ball.
efrigerate at least 30 minutes before using. Thinly line tiny tartlet (1 to
½ inches) tins.

for filling:
teaspoon lemon juice
teaspoon vanilla
stick butter
dash salt
cup light karo
½ cups chopped pecans
cup sugar
large eggs, beaten

rown butter in saucepan until golden brown - DO NOT BURN, let cool.
separate bowl add other ingredients in order listed, mixing after each
ldition. Add cooled butter last and spoon into unbaked tartlet shell. Bake
or 25 minutes in 350* oven. Cool in tins on racks, loosen with tip and turn
it on rack to cool completely. Yield 8 doz tassies or 1 pie.

**To make pecan pie, pour into unbaked pie shell and bake at 425* for
minutes, then lower temperature to 325* for 45 minutes.
***Pecan tassies freeze well and are great to pull out of the freezer ar
thaw for picnics!

Bowl Scraper

As I stand in the kitchen making holiday cookies
I carefully portion out the batter and as I clean the bowl
ears unexpectedly surface and pour into the bowl, washing away the
spicy cookie dough
n almost empty bowl that was once filled with love and eagerly awaited
by warm little fingers
I thank God for my memories
shall never stop looking every holiday season for that happy little child
in my kitchen…
I will forever miss my little bowl scraper.

Order Form

Please send me_____copies @ $29.95 each, $_____

Name_____

Address_____

City/State/Zip_____

Alabama residents please add 4% sales tax on books_____

Postage and handling _____ copies @ $3.50 1st book _____

($1.50 each additional book)_____

Total amount enclosed_____

Enclosed is my check payable to: Betty Ruth's Kitchen

Mail orders to:

      Betty Ruth's Kitchen
      P.O. Box 109
      Point Clear, Al 36564

      or Email amsac@gyne.com

      or order on my website http://www.gyne.com

      or call 251-990-9161

Index

Cheese Olive Balls, 16

Cheese Sauce, 270

cheesecake

    Basil Pesto Cheesecake, 11

    Pumpkin Cheesecake, 344

cherries

    Curried Fruit Bake, 264

chicken. *See also* chicken breasts; chicken livers

    Chicken Curry, 138

    Chicken Grandmere, 140

    Chicken Tagine with Olives and Preserved Lemons, 141

    Coq au Vin, 147

    Hot Chicken Salad, 80

    Jamaican Jerk Chicken, 150

    Mr. Glenn Stanley's Brissled Chicken, 144

    Paella, 106

    Pasta Shells with Chicken Salad, 30

    Penne Puttanesca with Chicken, 303

    The Phantom Cook's Cold Chicken Roulade, 154

    Rum Point Chicken in Coconuts, 152

chicken breasts

    Chicken Breasts with Dried Beef, 148

    Chicken Cordon Bleu, 151

    Chicken Piccata, 145

    Feta Chicken Breasts, 146

    Goat Cheese Chicken Rolls, 149

    Jamaican Jerk Chicken, 150

    Poulet en Papillote, 143

Chicken Cordon Bleu, 151

Chicken Curry, 138

Chicken Grandmere, 140

chicken livers

    Chicken Livers in Red Wine, 155

    Stonewall Chicken Livers, 156

Chicken Piccata, 145

G

game. *See* poultry and game

Garides Me Feta (Shrimp Soup), 47

Gazpacho, 43

Gazpacho Filled Avocado, 79

Ginger-Yogurt Dressing, 280

gingerbread, 355

Gingersnap Crust with Lemon Ice Cream, 360

Glazed Fruit Tartlets, 340

goat cheese

    Asparagus with Goat Cheese and Walnuts, 67

    Goat Cheese and Sun-Dried Tomato Tartines, 17

    Goat Cheese Chicken Rolls, 149

    Goat Cheese in Grape Leaves with Tomato and Olive Salad, 7

    tea sandwiches, 309

Graham Glover's Biscuits, 328

grains, *See also*, bulgur, barley, rice, wild rice, quinoa

    Asparagus Risotto II, 285

    Barley and Mushroom Casserole, 289

    Basic Polenta, 287

    BRS Jalapeño Cheese Grits, 284

    Bulgur Pilaf, 291

    Curried Rice Pilaf, 293

    My Wild Rice Casserole, 294

    Peter Devin's Risotto, 286

    Pilaf from La Cuisine Classique, 290

    Wild Mushroom Risotto, 288

    Wild Rice and Toasted Pecan Pilaf, 292

Granola Banana-Nut Bread, 321

grape leaves

    Goat Cheese in Grape Leaves with Tomato and Olive Salad, 7

grapefruit

    Avocado and Grapefruit Salad, 60

    Baked Grapefruit Alaska, 331

pastries
    Creamed Seafood in Puff Pastry Fish, 102
    Janie's Ice Box Rolls, 326
    Pate Brisee II, 327
pâté
    Braunsweiger Peppercorn Pâté, 5
peaches
    Chutney Baked Peaches, 261
    Curried Fruit Bake, 264
Pear Halves Filled with Mint, 256
pears
    Curried Fruit Bake, 264
    Pear Halves filled with Mint, 256
    Pears Baked with Blue Cheese and Port, 257
peas. *See* black-eyed peas; green peas
pecans
    Pecan Pralines, 366
    Pecan Tassies, 336, 367
    Spicy Pecans, 3
    Wild Rice and Toasted Pecan Pilaf, 292
Peeper's Peepers Corned Beef with Nested Eggs, 94
Penne Puttanesca with Chicken, 303
Persillade, 276
Pesto Meatloaf, 176
Pesto Torte, 29
Peter Devin's Risotto, 286
The Phantom Cook's Cold Chicken Roulade, 154
Pheasant with Wild Mushrooms, 164
Picnic Pasta Salad, 83
pie crust
    Pate Brisee II, 327
pies
    Chocolate Chess Pie, 357
    Gingersnap Crust with Lemon Ice Cream, 360
    Kahlúa, Fudge, and Macadamia Pie, 365